Kitchen Tables
& Other Midlife Musings

Niela Eliason

papier-mache

135 Aviation Way #14
Watsonville, CA 95076

04 03 02 01 00 99 98 97 96 95 94   10 9 8 7 6 5 4 3 2 1

ISBN: 0-918949-62-9 Softcover

Ceramic art on cover by Judy Miller
Cover design by Cynthia Heier
Photo by Richard T. Eliason

Grateful acknowledgment is made to the following publications which first published some of the material in this book:

Evening Independent, St. Petersburg, Florida; *St. Petersburg Times,* St. Petersburg, Florida; *Bradenton Herald,* Bradenton, Florida; *Hers* magazine, Longboat Key, Florida; and *St. Petersburg Masters Swim Program Newsletter,* St. Petersburg, Florida.

Library of Congress Cataloging-in-Publication Data

Eliason, Niela, 1930-
        Kitchen tables (and other midlife musings) / Niela Eliason.
            p.   cm.
        ISBN 0-918949-62-9
        1. Middle aged women—Psychology. 2. Middle age—Psychological aspects.   I. Title.
HQ1059.4.E38 1994
305.24'4—dc20   94-41414
                                                                     CIP

 This book is printed on acid-free, recycled paper containing a minimum of 85 percent total recycled fiber with 15 percent postconsumer, de-inked fiber.

To Dick
and to my other teachers
Steven Eliason, George Eliason, Davadene Barker, Charles Hirsch,
Jeanne Grinstead, Dan Wells, Harriet Deer, Bob Hall, and Fred Wright,
and the Saturday morning writers group, especially Susan Brown,
Pamela Peters, and Rhoda Bader.

We are the old women,
We are the new women.
We are the same women,
Wiser than before.
　　　　—Croning Ceremony Chant

◆
Contents

Kitchen Tables

Through no fault of my own, I have become middle-aged. It's not a character flaw, it's just something that happened when I wasn't paying attention—while I was going back to college, or finding work at a newspaper as a freelance writer, or cleaning out the grown kids' rooms and suddenly discovering a room of my own, one which sprouted a typewriter and later a computer. And on the way, I grew from a chronic reader to a writer and now am disgruntled because I don't have as much time to read.

I am sitting at a small black-granite table, a shelf really, in my kitchen. The table is suitable for telephoning or making grocery lists. I sit there with a cup of double-caffeine coffee (reading isn't my only bad habit) and think about kitchen tables past.

By the time we are fifty and sixty, we've sat at a lot of kitchen tables. We can trace the years through our kitchen tables.

One of ours was a hand-me-down white enamel with leaves on the sides to pull out or to slide under if we didn't need them. Another was white-painted wood with carved legs. It came from the Goodwill store, which was our interior design center in 1954.

I remember eating lunch at that table. Peanut butter sandwiches were popular with the five-year-old lunch crowd in 1960. I wondered if I would ever have a grown-up conversation again. I did, of course. Every two or three days, my medical student husband would get off duty from the emergency room and come home. We'd sit at the kitchen table, and he'd try to talk even though he hadn't had enough sleep in the last three days. Sometimes he'd fall asleep at the table.

The dog had puppies under the kitchen table one Christmas Eve, and nobody believed my claim that it was a virgin birth.

The kitchen table is where I tried to make my own hospital nursing schedule mesh with the available baby-sitters. The sitters had to be grandmas or friends. Paid sitters were not in the budget. That was before the Women's Movement. When I began to read that women should have their own careers, I wondered what the big deal was. I'd been buying the groceries for ten years.

Kitchen tables aren't like dining room tables. Nothing important happens at the dining room table. Only superficial things like company, or Christmas, or roast leg of lamb. No decisions were made at the dining room table. We were a kind of pretend family there. But if we were going to have a family fight, we'd have it at the dining room table. In the kitchen, we talked as contemporaries. In the dining room, there was a pecking order. So I began serving dinner in the kitchen, and we all got along a lot better.

Women used to visit in each other's kitchens. My friend, Shirl, and I used to sit with cups of coffee and talk in a sunny kitchen, folding the laundry while our toddlers played around our feet. I don't think women do that very much anymore. More of them are at work now, and answering machines do the talking. Years later, Shirl wrote to me: "Your newspaper columns are just like talking to you. It's as if we are sitting down and having a chat, like we used to do." After that, when the writing was advancing slowly, I would pretend I was talking to Shirl, and the writing would go better.

Twenty-five years ago, in a suburban kitchen with a built-in Formica table, I sat with a little six-inch television set and watched a man walk on the moon. The same week, I sat there and read about Chappaquiddick on the front page of the *St. Petersburg Times*. I think our world changed *that* week, not the week John Kennedy was killed.

The kitchen table is where I crammed for an American literature test in 1977. And when I threw my algebra book against the wall because I couldn't make the numbers work, my youngest son, also a college student by that time, helped me—the same son who made me laugh by reading the comics at the kitchen table, complete with accents and dramatics. In 1980, at the age of fifty, I hung my college diploma over the kitchen table.

Recently, with the children grown, my husband and I found a smaller, just-right house and are comfortably dug in. As soon as I walked into it, I knew it was my house, the one for which I'd waited for years. It has just one flaw. The kitchen is too small for a table.

We still hang out there though, leaning against the counter, eating Wheat Thins right out of the box while we wait for the water to boil for the spaghetti. We talk as much as ever.

Finishing my coffee, I think about how the kitchen is still a gathering place, a source of emotional as well as physical nourishment. Talking in the kitchen is a tradition. In fact, why don't you pull up a chair, and I'll make a fresh pot of coffee.

Women's Friendships

Some midlife women have had their friends longer than they've had their husbands. Some of them like their friends better than their husbands. In their book, *Women and Friendship*, Dr. Joel D. Block and Diane Greenberg report sociologist Robert Bell's study in which women discuss the three people with whom they most like to spend time. Sixty-four percent of the women interviewed named their husband, 67 percent named a mother or daughter, and a whopping *98 percent* named a woman friend. Women have always formed close friendships and shared the large and small events of their lives with each other. They comfort and inspire each other.

I read somewhere that younger people—thirtysomethings—are poor lovers, poor spouses, and poor parents, but are excellent friends. Maybe that's because they spend so much time at work—which becomes their social life and emotional support system—while their at-home time is spent trying to keep up with laundry, getting something to eat, bathing the children, and falling into bed exhausted.

When we married in the 1940s and 1950s, we gave up our school and work friends, especially if we quit working soon after marriage as was common then. Instead, we adopted the wives of our husband's friends as our friends. We didn't always have much in common with these marriage friends. We pretended that planning the bridge club potluck supper was important, but, in fact, the excitement was manufactured. One or two of these women, however, would become our good and intimate friends.

About the time men began wearing their hair long, women began making choices. One of these choices was to drop garden club and go back to school. There, we found friends of our own with common interests. These new friends were separate from our marriage friends. This was heady stuff, kind of like being in the dorm again.

And then a funny thing would happen. We'd go back home for a class reunion and there would be our old best friend, our college roommate, or one of our bridesmaids. The friendship would resume with glad cries, and conversations would take up where they had left off, as if no time had passed.

One woman told me about an old college roommate who came to visit. They sat up late talking. "My four daughters were enchanted," she said. "They wouldn't go to bed. 'Mom,' they said, 'we've never seen you so young.'"

Women's friendships survive distance and long periods of conversational drought. When we meet an old friend again, we find that we have changed in similar ways. We've resigned from the choir, taken up yoga, and taken a job. We've adjusted to seeing single parents listed in newspaper birth announcements. We both wear glasses, use a computer, and wish we had a fax machine. We've each had our colors done, and neither of us wears beige anymore. It's eerie to find that although we are different people than we were thirty years ago, we have grown to be alike once again without comparing our thoughts in the interval.

By the time we're fifty, we've had even our new friends for ten or twenty years. I know of two women who have been good friends, sharing common interests, family news, and their social life for years. They decided to go into business together and began a successful flower shop. This sort of thing can test a friendship, what with the daily togetherness and business crises. But their friendship only blossomed.

"We get along well," one of them said, "because, although we share each other's lives, we still respect each other's privacy."

And that might be the secret to women's long-lasting friendships.

Moving

I saw my friend, Joan, at the supermarket last week. We jockeyed our grocery carts for position to be first at the back of the store where the empty boxes are kept. Each of us was planning a transition. We were both getting ready to move to smaller places.

"Don't you just love moving?" asked Joan. We were both exhilarated with rummaging through closets and discarding things. We felt a sense of escape and renewal. Men, we agreed, generally do not feel the same way. They seem to look back and regret what was not done, not fully enjoyed, while women look forward and think the best is yet to come.

We lived in our big old suburban family home for twenty years. We laughed and cried, and loved and quarreled. We celebrated and suffered Christmases and head colds, school buses, birthdays, colleges, and barbecues. Our sons grew from grade-schoolers to adults. The old neighborhood changed from people with teenagers and adult children to younger parents with small children.

I am still not completely unpacked. As I write this, I remain at the mercy of city inspectors, painters, and plumbers, but I love my smaller house downtown and have faith that, in time, I will find a place for the big soup pot, locate my address book, and install a towel bar in the bathroom. The cat might even come out from under the bed.

I called Joan a few days after her move to a condominium. She said she felt sentimental about leaving her old home, "But buildings don't have memories. Material things are not memories. The memories are within us. I feel that I am moving from one life space to another."

But she did cry once. "I put my children's baby books, *my* baby book, the signed books from my mother's and father's funerals, and two ongoing family photo albums in a single box. I felt as though I had put a hundred years of history into one box. Even my mother-in-law, a strong woman, cried over the move. I think it represented a change to her, too. Because of moving," she said, "I feel that I know myself better, know my history."

The process of handling everything we own stirs up memories, memories that would continue to lie dormant as long as photo albums and baby pictures lay packed in a box on the top shelf of the closet. My husband, who is a dedicated pack rat and has not thrown out anything for thirty-five years, saved our very first book of check stubs from 1953. Check #001 was for tuition, the next for flowers, and the third for groceries. I want to think those checks are symbolic of the essence of life: education (work), love, and pleasures, although not necessarily in that order.

Moving also helps us notice the things that have surrounded us every day for so long. One morning, before we left our old house, my husband called my attention to the dawn colors over Tampa Bay. "It's a beautiful sunrise," he said, with wonder in his voice.

"The sun has been coming up beautifully over the water for the last twenty years," I responded, truthfully but unkindly, as is unfortunately my way, "but you didn't take time to look at it."

"I thought there'd always be another," he said.

Now that the days of viewing unobstructed sunrises over the water from our old house became finite—just as the numbers of sunrises in life are finite—they became more dear, but we don't think about our sunrises until a major transition makes us notice that time is passing.

If I didn't learn anything else from moving (such as don't acquire so much), I did learn the importance of seizing the day—work, love, enjoy. Now.

History in the Recipe Box

Jan Johnson called recently and asked for the Pillsbury Bake-Off zucchini pie recipe that I had given her years ago. She couldn't find hers.

I met Jan on a student tour to Spain during our college days. She was a guitar-strumming nineteen-year-old then. Now she is a publicist for a chalet in Florida.

Her call made me realize that I have tucked away many memories under the file headings of meats and entrees, cakes, salads, and sauces in my recipe box. The box seems to hold our family history.

There's the pumpkin chiffon pie recipe from Pat Carney. She was the commanding officer's wife when we were stationed in the Philippine Islands. That was in 1961, and it is still the only recipe I use for pumpkin pie. Pat served the pie after a curry dinner, and it was just the right ending for that menu. After dinner we played charades. Now we don't even have navy bases in the Philippines, much less dinner parties.

And there's my mother's recipe for dumplings. She dropped the mixture into stewed chicken, and it was so good. I can't even remember the last time I ate dumplings at Mama's house.

And Hope Attridge's pound cake, the only cake that I've ever been able to make successfully. This recipe goes back to Denver in 1959. The recipe is written on the back of a telephone notepad and is all brown and spotted. I had to stick it onto a recipe card with a glue stick so it wouldn't disintegrate. I like to keep the original copies. My handwriting has changed over the years, and the recipe looks very young. It tells me that I was very young once, too.

You can see changes in food fashions in a recipe box. No more recipes for macaroni, hamburger, and tomato soup casseroles. No more tuna noodle with mushroom soup, either. In fact, the whole casseroles section of my card file is completely empty. Now there are recipes for things like bean salads and pasta with vegetables.

Here's a new recipe: Hillary Rodham Clinton's chocolate chip cookies. I haven't tried that yet.

But look, Emerita Cooper's Spanish rice, 1961. Emerita was a Filipina married to an American engineer. She didn't know how to cook American food when she married, so her husband bought her *The Fannie Farmer Cookbook*. By the time I met Emerita, she was the best cook I'd encountered. She taught me to make pie crust with instructions such as, ". . . three big spoonfuls of Crisco," and, "It should feel like this when you crumble it." She also told me that a roast should be put on at four o'clock. If it were just family, the roast would be small and would be done at dinner time. If you had company, the roast would be larger and dinner would be served later. Oddly enough, it works. I wonder where Emerita is now.

Bernice Feagans' cole slaw dressing is a family favorite. We were both on altar guild, and our kids went to school together. Here, I'll give you Bernice's cole slaw dressing recipe.

Cole Slaw Dressing

2 tablespoons sugar	2 tablespoons vinegar
1/2 teaspoon mustard or to taste	3 tablespoons milk

Mix these well and add three big globs of mayonnaise. Stir well and add to about a half a head of shredded cabbage.

So many memories, so many people, so many events are tucked in my file. I got kind of lost looking for the old zucchini pie recipe for Jan. Maybe we should call it the reminiscence box instead of the recipe box.

The Chicken Soup Myth

Chicken soup is about the only thing left that we can trust. Milk, once a wholesome food and good for you, now has to have its lethal fat skimmed out. The classic American bacon and eggs breakfast has become abhorrent to decent cholesterol and nitrite fearing people. You can't even trust coffee anymore.

But, so far, for no discernible reason, you can still trust chicken soup. I can't think of a single healthy reason for eating a dead bird that is every bit as undiscriminating a scavenger as the shrimp that eat the dreck from the bottom of the sea. Chickens will eat anything. I know. My mother used to keep chickens in a low building behind the house, and I saw what they ate. We won't go into it here. (As an aside, my mother was embarrassed that I named the chickens after her church friends—Irene, Dorothy, Mrs. Evans, and so on.)

In spite of the fact that chicken soup is made of greasy dead birds with filthy habits, offering chicken soup is our first reflex when things go wrong and we need strength and comfort.

When my daughter-in-law was hospitalized with a serious illness, I rushed to the kitchen and got a chicken out of the freezer. I knew she would not be able to eat the soup. She was not allowed to have anything by mouth except ice chips; she was nourished by intravenous fluid. No matter. Our generation knows that when people are sick, you make chicken soup.

I called my son to say I was bringing soup. Even though his wife couldn't eat it, at least it would keep up *his* strength.

"Ma," he pleaded, "please don't bring chicken soup. The freezer is full of it."

Somebody beat me to it.

But what do I know about chicken soup? I'm not even Jewish. I called my friend, Bernice, the rabbi's wife. She said Jewish people might not make the best chicken soup, but they probably make the most.

She put dill and parsley in hers. I put lemon and a tiny bit of sugar in mine. The lemon has the added value of vitamin C. The fact that vitamin C is destroyed by cooking doesn't bother me a bit. We agreed that boned and skinned chicken breast will not do to make soup. It won't have any flavor. You have to use whole chickens. The fat can be skimmed off later.

Bernice believed strongly in the healing powers of chicken soup. "It's healthful, warm, soothing, and is given with love," she said. "Chicken soup is sometimes called Jewish penicillin."

I had heard chicken soup called "buba-myecin." *Buba* means grand-mother in Hebrew, and *myecin* refers to antibiotics. Bernice thought I was talking about *buba meises*, grandmother's stories. A shouted three-way conversation for clarification among Bernice, the rabbi, and me ensued. After a lot of confusion, we gave up.

The chicken soup myth is international. My people were Nordic; my daughter-in-law is of Polish, French, and Italian ancestry; and Bernice referred to herself as Jewish-American. We all believe in chicken soup.

I'm staying with my original statement. You can trust chicken soup.

Leftovers

I don't do dinner very well, but I'm good at salads, soups, and sandwiches. This is partly because I'm cooking for two instead of for a family, and partly because we eat more simply now. We used to have a lot of roasts, fried meats, and potatoes, or casseroles made with noodles. We said noodles, not pasta. Today, pasta with some lightly cooked vegetables takes the place of all those casseroles.

About the time my children were growing up, the empty nest syndrome was fashionable. Warnings were rampant about the difficulty of this period of life. I seemed to have missed it all around. My children were grown for two years when one day I realized that I hadn't remembered to be lonely and sad. But then, I've never been a very trendy person. Three years behind is about average for me. By the time I figure out what's happening, it's over.

One of the frights about the empty nest syndrome concerned cooking. My mother moaned about how difficult it was to cook for two— recipes were too big, there were too many leftovers, and so on.

As usual I wasn't paying attention to maternal instructions. Instead, I thought cooking for two was an oasis of leisure time. I still cook in the same quantities—most recipes are for four. This means we have one meal plus lunch or a cache of prepared food in the freezer, making my life easy another day. I love leftovers. The only way I can bear the two-day Thanksgiving marathon is by thinking of the noncooking days that will follow. I do so many creative leftovers, my husband suggested we open a restaurant and call it Leftover's.

During the empty nest period of my life, our sons would come home to live from time to time. That might explain why I never suffered as poignantly as I should have. One time, a microwave oven came home also, and I tried that for a period of three or four months. I learned that it takes longer and requires more attention to cook rice in a microwave than it does in a pot on the stove. After several earnest experiments, I decided the microwave was mostly useful for thawing frozen things, and when it left with our son I was glad to have my counter space back and have never wanted a microwave oven since.

A newspaper article told about the difficulty of writing recipes today. If the instructions say to "Blend butter and sugar, then add one egg," the modern cook is likely to throw it all into the blender and whirl it. The act of blending must now be described in detail.

Not long ago, I made an apple pie for a special occasion, and while I was doing it, holding up the pie plate and cutting off the excess dough from the edge with a paring knife, I thought about how my mother had done it exactly the same way. I thought about my pastry blender with bent blades and all the paint worn off the handle. It used to be red.

I don't like to cook as much as I used to, and I enjoy the simpler things more. We eat less red meat, but I still make my mother-in-law's meat loaf from time to time. The recipe calls for 1/4 cup of horseradish, which seems like an error but isn't. You can't identify the flavor. It just tastes good.

Marian's Meat Loaf

2 pounds ground beef   1 onion, chopped
1 cup oatmeal   2 eggs, beaten
3/4 cup tomato juice   2 teaspoons salt
2 teaspoons paprika   1 teaspoon dry mustard
1/4 cup horseradish

Mix all ingredients together. Place in loaf pan and spread 1/2 cup ketchup over top. Bake at 375 degrees for 1-1/2 hours.

It's a big recipe. There's enough for meat loaf sandwiches the next day and another portion to put in the freezer. I wish I had some meat loaf in the freezer today.

---◆---

Labor Day

After years of being responsible for the care and well-being, health, and growth of small people,

After years of never going to the bathroom by ourselves, never having a solitary bath, never locking the bathroom door,

After tennis lessons, swim lessons, Cub Scouts, Indian Guides, and then drum lessons,

After drying tears, bandaging knees, nursing pneumonia, removing splinters from fingers and one from the bottom,

After years of teacher conferences, report cards, trips to the orthodontist and to the library for homework research unannounced until the last moment,

After solving quarrels, bolstering self-esteem, finding their shoes and their sunglasses, and paying their college tuition,

Now we're supposed to mind our own business? Let them make their own decisions? Even when it's clear they're going to hurt themselves?

Now we're supposed to let go?

Second Parenthood

Someone said we are given children to test us and to make us more spiritual. If this is true, some parents must be sainted by now. They have tolerated the terrible twos, survived the sassy sixteens, and endured the contentious twenties. Then they are tested once again by the same children trucking home with backpacks and cardboard boxes, wanting to stay a couple of weeks until they find work, finish school, get a divorce, or even raise their own children. Just when parents thought they were home free, the children are back at the door, whining to be let in.

A friend told me that her son, a postgraduate student, called to say he and his pregnant wife wanted to come home for just a few months, while he finished school.

"I'm panicked," my friend said. "The baby is due in a month. I don't want to baby-sit. I've got my part-time accounting job, my tennis, and my museum volunteer work. I've got my own life. I don't think I ever liked babies, anyway." She has a big house with plenty of room. "I love my kids," she said, "but I'm getting tired of this."

In spite of her outspoken spontaneity, her three grown children know they are welcome. At least, they've never hesitated to come home to live from time to time. My friend's advice to parents whose children are grown, is: "Buy a one-bedroom house."

A sixtyish man said, "Two adult males can't live in the same house. When I was twenty-seven, I married and brought my wife to live in my parents' five-room apartment. After nine months, my father said, 'I'm tired of living in *your* house. You've got to move.' He paid a deposit on an apartment for us in the same building."

Moving back home often makes a great deal of sense for the children. It can cost more than a thousand dollars to set up a modest apartment with first and last month's rent, security, electricity, and telephone deposits. There are many homeless people today, and the lack of family to help them is a contributing problem.

Grown children coming home to live was not common in the 1950s, but today "boomerang babies" are becoming part of our culture. Parents know that adult children who temporarily return to the nest are in distress or they wouldn't be there. These children need encouragement and love, sometimes help with alcohol or drug problems, or time to regroup with further education or training.

Having grown children living at home again often offers an opportunity to solidify family relationships. Parents and child might have had some stormy times during the naturally rebellious adolescent years, but when the child comes home after being on his or her own for a time, the relationship is different. The parents and offspring become reacquainted as adults. It can be a time of healing. The family members find that they like—as well as love—each other. They become friends.

One mother said she did not want to be awakened by phone calls saying the young person will be coming in late—or not at all. "I'm not on patrol anymore," she said.

Another said, "Even though my daughter is grown and has lived alone for several years, I still cannot sleep until the porch light goes off."

The parenting bond is a strong one. Even when it's broken, it reconnects itself quickly. It's hard to learn that we, as parents, can't be everything to everybody—forever.

Old Enough to Know Better

Life . . . begins when the kids leave home and the dog dies.
—Unknown

Some women over sixty are dismantling their highly desirable state in life by deliberately having late-life babies. They're old enough to know better.

Martin Mull said that having children is like having a bowling alley installed in your brain. I don't know who Mull is, but I agree with him. I'm not alone in marveling at the news that older women are choosing to bear children. A fifty-nine-year-old English woman gave birth to twins. A sixty-one-year-old Italian woman announced her pregnancy.

It is now possible, by artificial insemination, for postmenopausal women to become pregnant. By tinkering in petri dishes with donor eggs of a younger woman and the father's sperm, a pregnancy is conceived and transplanted into the mother's uterus. Science triumphs over nature once again. Or is it a mistake? There are mixed notices on this one.

Not many women in their sixties would volunteer for the ultimate endurance test of raising a child, but, on the other hand, who's to say a vigorous sixty-year-old wouldn't make a good parent? Often we hear older women say how much they enjoy their grandchildren. (Others say grandparents and grandchildren get along so well because they have a common enemy.) Conversely, young people, capable of conceiving without requiring the kindness of strangers, sometimes do a lousy job of parenting.

Dissident voices are heard are on the subject.

"Women do not have the right to have a child," yelps British Health

Secretary Virginia Bottomley. "The child has a right to a suitable home."

But when an older man fathers a child, usually with a younger woman, he is congratulated and regarded as being rather cunning. No mention is made of a father's "right" to a latter-day child.

Many older women and men raise their grandchildren because their children cannot or will not do it. Maybe these older parents will be good parents because they have years of experience and maturity behind them. At a time of life when they are self-confident, possibly financially secure, and probably enjoying some spare time, the older parents might be better equipped for child care than in their younger years. People are maintaining their health and vigor later into life. Sixty used to be old, but it isn't anymore. The sixty-year-old in good health today is as capable as a forty-year-old.

Some people are concerned about the physical demands of an older woman carrying a pregnancy full-term. This is a valid concern. As I recall, however, pregnancy lasts only nine months and was the easy part of parenthood. The real work begins when the baby comes home. Have the older parents forgotten the agony of months of sleep deprivation? Don't forget the spilled cereal, the diaper contents, the whining, and the living room that looks like a branch office for Toys "R" Us. There is the lack of one's own identity. Mothers are mothers. They belong to their children and not to themselves. Or so it seems at the time. And those car seats. Getting a child in and out of the car requires the strength of a sumo wrestler. Ask a local grandmother.

When this child is ten, the mother will be seventy. At seventy-five, the mother will be suffering teenage rebellion. These women will be eighty when their child is college age—if they survive to see it.

Why would anyone want to go through this trauma when they could be resting on their retirement funds? This desire to have another child might be a carry over from the prefeminist days of the post-World

War II era when women's primary goals were to stay home, have babies, and take care of the house. Bored at thirty-five or forty, women would have another baby to give themselves a purpose in life, a reason to be, a feeling of youth (another requirement in those days: to always be young).

Not many women will choose to bear a child at sixty, but those who want to begin parenting again—or even for the first time—with the twenty-four-hour-a-day responsibility of being everything to everyone should have that privilege. It's not a right, but a choice and a privilege granted by modern technology. We have to recognize that it is now possible for older women to have children just as we accept abortion as a choice, just as we face the option of taking our own lives under certain circumstances.

Postmenopausal women who are informed about the physical dangers and requirements of childbearing and who plan for the possibility of their death before their child reaches adulthood should be allowed to choose pregnancy. Such a choice should not be a societal or bureaucratic one. The consequences must be assumed by the parents. I do not, however, think there will be a great demand for this service.

Boyfriends and Girlfriends

"My mother's boyfriend is coming for dinner," said a woman behind me in the check-out line. Once again, the feathers on the back of my head rose like Daisy Duck's, and I began to feel snippy. The inappropriate use of boyfriend and girlfriend has prickled my scalp for years. There are alternatives for these words. Friend for instance.

We all clearly understand the casual conversational use of boyfriend and girlfriend. These terms are, however, inappropriate and degrading, especially when used in print or on television to report the news. For instance, I read this recently: "A seventy-year-old woman was stabbed Friday during an argument with her boyfriend . . . sixty-six." These people are not children. And if they were once friends, they do not seem to be now. This couple was clearly past the age of being boy and girl, and the same is true of other younger adults in their twenties or thirties.

We understand that the terms refer to a romantic, intimate liaison, but using words in this way flouts style. Style, coming from the Latin *stylus*, is defined by *Webster's Third New International Dictionary* as a writing tool or a mode of expressing thought in oral or written language. The dictionary runs with this idea for half of a column giving other interesting definitions and uses such as: "the aspects of literary composition that are concerned with mode and form of expression as distinguished from content or message." An example is given: "His style is so graceful that one regrets he has nothing to say."

Even though the same dictionary defines girlfriend and boyfriend as the companion of a girl or boy, or a woman or man, the *style* of using those terms for adults defies logic. There are other choices. Friend and companion work well. How about acquaintance, confidant, intimate, comrade, colleague? Or if the parties are no longer friends, how about enemy or combatant?

Depending on the circumstances, there are also partner, associate, roommate, confrere, consort, sweetheart, sweet patootie, date, paramour, suitor, inamorata, man, woman, bedfellow, sugar daddy, gigolo, lover, mistress, fiancé, and much, much more to suit your style and meaning.

Staying Married

Marriage is a friendship recognized by the police.
—Robert Louis Stevenson

Two things I refuse to write about are sex and diets. Entirely too much has been said about both already. Do whatever you want to do, eat whatever you want to eat; just don't tell me about it, and I won't tell you.

Marriage and staying married, however, are something else. Staying married as a skill doesn't seem to be well-developed today. Some prefer disposable marriages to marriages that are maintained and repaired—just as it is easier today to buy a new telephone than to have the old one repaired. (The old phone might be only six months old.)

Like telephones, marriage is a matter of communication. In my marriage, we have always talked a lot. We've also interrupted each other a lot, quarreled, and had our share of problems.

The essence of a long-lasting marriage is friendship. If you don't like the person with whom you have breakfast, how can you possibly love him or her? That doesn't mean you have to agree with each other on everything. In fact, marriages and friendships are spicier and more fun if there are differences. For instance, my husband is an Episcopalian, and I'm an existentialist. He likes to ride horses, and I don't. He goes on vacations where he sits on a horse all day for five days. This is incomprehensible to me. I don't want to sit spraddle-legged on a neurotic animal that weighs twelve hundred pounds and bolts at nonexistent snakes in the grass. On the other hand, he has no interest in going to writers' conferences and listening to pale people belabor alliteration, foreshadowing, metaphors, and query letters.

But we both like to go to Mexico and just mess around. All of this makes life twice as interesting as it would be if both of us did exactly the same things, went to the same places, knew the same people. If we were just alike, our marriage would be flaccid.

There are other advantages to staying married. We remember the same old songs. Our song is "You Go to My Head." But he still gets annoyed if I loudly sing "It Had to Be You" by repeating the first phrase all the way through. It's the only song I know that you can do that with. We share the memory of traveling to the Philippines on an unair-conditioned navy ship and thinking it was a great adventure. It was.

But marriage is not all memories and sentiment. A lot of midlife women complain that they don't feel they are part of their husband's lives. There is nothing specifically wrong, there is just an emptiness. Some older men still feel that their spouse is more of a servant than a companion. They expect their wives to look pretty no matter what, provide dinner, be the laundry fairy, and be seen and not heard—that is, not to interrupt or have different opinions or interests. Many older women are going back to school, starting businesses of their own, or making new friends to supplement the lack of friendship at their own breakfast table.

Marriage is always a risk. Sometimes the most made-in-heaven liaison explodes, and the most unlikely duos are the ones with the most staying power.

Voltaire said, "Marriage is the only adventure open to the cowardly." Well maybe, but even if it takes more courage and stamina than running the bulls in Pamplona, it's worth the risk.

The Fiftieth Birthday

Life used to begin at forty. Today it begins at fifty or even later.

The fortieth birthday used to be the time for introspection and reevaluation, for wailing and gnashing of teeth, and for shaking one's fist at the gods. But nobody pays much attention to forty anymore. Forty is for baby boomers. The fiftieth birthday is now the demarcation point at which we have fewer years left than we already have lived.

People have various reactions to turning fifty.

Some sink into an indigo funk. They start moping months before the birthday party, suffering sleeplessness, depression, and blurred vision. Pale and whiny on the day of the party, they somehow survive the celebration, smiling wanly at their friends' hilarious jokes. The postparty funk might continue for several weeks after the birthday.

Some start rehearsing their own death. "If I die . . .," they'll begin. "What do you mean, *if?*" their friends say. But these funkers continue to worry about how and when they will join the angels. It might be necessary to point out to them that dying will be discussed at the appropriate time, but it does not entertain one's cohorts to suffer the possible variations daily for the next thirty years. Eventually someone at the lunch table at work will get tired of the moaning and the crestfallen face and point out brusquely that being fifty beats the alternative.

Others have an entirely different view. Some have a great soaring feeling of release and freedom. They feel like the phoenix, rising from the ashes, ready to start anew. "Okay," they think, "I did it. I survived being young and accomplished most of what I set out to do." With children raised and businesses stable, these birthday celebrants take a deep breath, look around them, and think: *The best is yet to come.* This is what they have worked and waited for.

Although it might not be perfect, life is as organized as it's going to get. There are still crises, but the time has come to do some of the things they always meant to do someday. And this is it—this is Someday. Now is the time to finish the college degree—or begin one. Learn to fly an airplane, or a kite. Make pottery, take acting lessons, join the Peace Corps, build a sand castle, play hooky, go to the movies in the afternoon.

By fifty, people have made enough mistakes to know that they are fallible—like everyone else—and that it's okay. They know they don't have to be perfect. They are less self-conscious. People who have been dying their hair for years let it grow out and are delighted to find that their natural grey is not only handsome, but the most flattering shade they can wear. Men revert to old favorite college styles that still feel comfortable and look good. They buy saddle shoes and V neck pullover sweaters.

With any luck at all, the children will have moved out, and the cupboard is bare of peanut butter and potato chips. They finally lose those extra pounds they've been carrying around for years. Or they say, the heck with it. Be a little plump.

People over fifty have a better sense of humor about minor irritations, but don't tolerate rudeness as gracefully as they used to. When the butcher says, "What's it going to be, young lady?" the midlife matron will respond, "I'll have four pork chops, please, sonny."

Life now begins at fifty because middle age lasts longer than it used to with people living longer and in good health. People used to survive only until sixty-five or so. They might have retired at fifty-five or sixty to enjoy their few remaining years quietly, reaping respect and solicitude from their children. But today, they feel the same as they did at forty, maybe better. They might not be as tired. Their adult children are part of two-paycheck families and haven't time to be solicitous, but in any case, the grandma who has a board meeting and a yoga class to attend hasn't got time to be patted on the head, anyway. That's not to say she wouldn't have time for a birthday party.

Croning Ceremonies: The Coming of Age

We are the old women, we are the new women.
We are the same women, wiser than before.

Crones are coming of age. There's a movement afoot to turn what has always been a negative into a positive. Many women fifty and older feel invisible. In the past, women beyond childbearing years have been considered useless, ugly, uninteresting.

Women across the country are shedding that image and using rituals called croning ceremonies to celebrate the time of "age, wisdom, and power," as Barbara Walker refers to it in her book, *The Crone*. Croning can be likened to a debut, but it is a true coming of age at the third stage of life.

"Croning," says Carolyn Taylor, fifty-four, who leads these rituals, "is meant to provide encouragement to women, a spiritual path to empowerment." The croning ceremony helps women become visible to themselves and to their circle of friends, giving them an authenticity. According to Taylor, "It is a time to come together, honoring and centering ourselves as women." Taylor adds that, "When women become fifty, they want to do something dramatic, something they haven't done before. It is the marking of a decision to make a change in your life yourself."

Ceremonies incorporate a variety of symbols and personal interests. Taylor leads with songs, chants, and drumming. She says anyone can lead the croning ritual, in fact, sometimes the women in the groups take over. Some women make a weekend of it, including birthday and divorce celebrations, cookouts, and walking on the beach. Although cronings are often held at night, under moonlight, I invited long-time friends to celebrate my coming of age in my urban living room on a cold winter morning. Some were crones, some pre-crones.

Led by Carolyn Taylor, a talking stick was passed around the circle of twelve women. The satin-ribboned wand gives the holder permission to speak without being interrupted. As each woman held the talking stick, she said something about herself and what was going on in her life. Whether they talked about their work or about their personal lives, the predominant theme was that of change and renewal. Taylor sees aging as a time of growth and the croning ceremony as a time to share your present, past, and future with the friends that you have.

After other symbolic rituals and music with the women joining in on drums, tambourines, and shakers, I was crowned as crone with a circle of woven ribbons, stars, and streamers.

I chose a new name for my coming of age: Persephone. I talked about the Persephone myth and how these ideas were incorporated in my own life. Persephone, among other things, offered the most possibility of growth of all the Greek goddesses. Growth and change are qualities I am seeking in my crone years. New names are not always part of the croning ceremony, and need not be mythical. Another woman chose Oak for her new name. How strong and calm that must make her feel.

The guests then talked about knowing me over the years. They spoke in warm and heartening terms but, more importantly, about the strength of the group which has met once a month for ten years.

I selected a Native American theme for my ceremony, using animal medicine cards. Each guest drew a card and interpreted her reading of it. I drew Bat, which told me to "Grow and become your future." Somehow, the cards always tell what you need to know.

At another croning, a woman who had very long hair wanted to make a change in her life and asked her friends to cut her hair as part of the ceremony. Another had many personal mementos—such as pictures and ceramic figurines—and passed them on to her friends as she started a new life. She let people choose what they wanted from her collection. At another ceremony, eight women were croned.

If possible, someone who has known the crone for a long time will attend and tell about the crone as a child or as an adult. It might be a relative or an old friend. Photos of the celebrant at the three stages of life (maiden, mother, and crone) are entertaining and draw appropriate—or inappropriate—remarks. Crones are noted for their clear perceptions—a childlike quality—and are often bawdy. In an essay called "The Artist After Fifty" Taylor writes, "The innocence of childhood seems to return with the crone years."

After the closing song and drumming, "We are the old women," we had a self-blessing, and then we lunched on salads and breads everyone brought. A cake had been decorated with pomegranate seeds to symbolize the Persephone myth. Gifts were opened—a poem written for the occasion, books, bumper stickers—and then all the crones went home happy, planning ceremonies of their own. Neighbors had complained about the noise—a good omen, we thought.

"Coming into the wisewoman age is almost as if you are flying, taking off," Taylor says. In an essay, "Goddesses, Cowgirls and Wildwomen," she writes, "Women are growing, mentally and emotionally leaving their nests . . . women with wings."

"In my forties," she said, "I wove nests. In my fifties, I'm making wings."

Back to School

I've always felt that September, not January, is the beginning of the new year. I know why this is. The new school year starts in September.

In Denver, where I grew up, the September air would become chilly and crisp after Labor Day. We'd have to wear sweaters in the late afternoon. Even the light seemed to change, becoming golden and hazy with motes, perhaps because of leaves burning all over town. We didn't think much about air pollution then.

The excitement of a new school year was fraught with anxiety as well as anticipation. Would we like our teacher? More important, would she like us? Could we do the work? Would we have friends? And *when* would we buy our Big Chief tablet and Ticonderoga pencils? And new shoes. It was a big deal when we started junior high school and had to have a gym suit, even if it was an ugly maroon and baggy.

Later in life, when I was married, my husband seemed to go to school forever, advancing through the undergraduate years and then graduate work. Except for three years in the navy, he didn't have a job for the first fifteen years we were married. A new year began each fall when he started a new round of education. Often that included moving as well.

So the beginning of the school year has been a big part of my orientation, always a new cycle, a rebirth in the fall. I never quite get over the excitement, just as I never stop looking forward to the mail. The anticipation of something new, something interesting, remains. I go back to school myself from time to time. And I still have a box of crayons in my desk drawer—in case of emergencies, like the grandchildren coming to visit.

All of that comes back to me when I see the ads for back-to-school clothes and supplies. The newspapers are full of them, and on television today there are ads sponsored by office supply stores. We used to buy our Big Chief tablets at the dime store. It's just as well. I would have gone berserk in an office supply store. I love office and school supplies.

One of the things I noticed about the television ads for office supplies for school children was the inference that good equipment would make one a good student. Success is linked to stuff. If you have a pencil case with pictures of dinosaurs or favorite cartoon characters, you will be a happy, successful student. I like that idea. I don't think it's true, but I like it anyway.

Over the years I have accumulated—in addition to crayons—a stapler, a postage scale, and a ruler, as well as an answering machine, green paper clips, several pens (black ink, never blue, throw out the blues if you accidentally fall heir to one), two of those wire in-out baskets, and some yellow happy-face stickers. I have a computer, but keep the old IBM Selectric II for envelopes because the printer glues envelopes shut. I get very agitated in an office supply store. There's hardly anything I need anymore. And I'm too stingy to duplicate what I already have.

At this point, one could make a good case for saying that by our middle years we've already enjoyed most of the excitements of life, and now we can just sit around while our Post-it notes dry out and lose their sticky. Not so. No matter how old we get, most of us still respond to the onset of fall and the new school year. We still sniff the cooler air and wonder what lies ahead.

Last week, I signed up for a junior college adult education class. Maybe I should go to the office supply store. I will, of course, need a new notebook. And one of those neon chartreuse highlighter pens might be just the thing to help me study. Yeah.

Girl Scout Cookies

The cookie agents are at large again. Several years ago, the Girl Scouts had a cookie box that interested me.

As usual, I bought a box of cookies that year and ate six before dinner and three after. I like the traditional trefoils. On one side of the box was written, "I'm not like anyone else." I liked that idea.

The Girl Scouts was the first organized women's group from which I resigned. My mother urged me to join rather than spend so much time reading *The Bobbsey Twins*. ("If you don't stop that reading, you're going to ruin your eyes!") In Girl Scouts, I learned that I wasn't like anyone else and didn't like to be pocketed with a group.

Unfortunately, I did not resign from the Girl Scouts until my mother had already bought all the parts of the uniform for me. First, she bought the neckerchief and the book. I think it was called *Merit Achievements Book* or something like that. It told how to earn badges. I didn't need or want any badges. Later she bought the beret and then the sage green uniform dress, complete with webbed belt.

My Scout troop worked on earning the cooking merit badge. It seemed a dull session, but I enjoyed earning the first-aid badge. In fact, years later I became a nurse. When the Scout leader asked if anyone had suggestions for other activities, I raised my hand and said I thought we ought to be "militaristic." I thought since we wore uniforms, we ought to do things like march and put up the school flag. I wasn't requesting combat, just some flag duty.

The scout leader said, "What?" Then she asked if anyone else had suggestions. She was a soft, motherly sort of woman. The other girls looked at me with hostile expressions. It wasn't long after that I resigned. When I told my mother, she sighed and looked at me with her arms folded over her chest and one eyebrow raised. She had just received the bill from the May Company for the dress and belt. I was ten then.

Looking on the other side of the Girl Scout cookie box, I read, "We have a lot in common." You bet we have. We have our femaleness and our wanting to be healthy and look good. We have our need to be respected and loved for who we are and what we do, whether we are bankers or housekeepers, teachers or truck drivers.

It's the "doing your own thing" as they say, that is common to us all. It is the salt that flavors our individuality. We learn to grow and change as the years go by, but we stay the same, still keeping some little-girl qualities about us (our innate tendency to anarchism, for instance).

It's good that some people like to be Girl Scouts and see that there are cookies for sale. I'm not like anyone else, but I'm glad that some people like to be organized, and I admire and envy their togetherness and the products of their togetherness.

When the doorbell rings and there are bright, excited little salesgirls piping in their singsong voices, "Would you like to buy some Girl Scout cookies?" I say, "Yes, yes, yes, I love Girl Scout cookies." If I miss the Scouts at home, I catch up with them at the supermarket.

I notice these Girl Scouts don't always have complete uniforms as we used to. They dress however they please, in whatever style is theirs. They seem to be much more sure of themselves. They also seem to be having a lot more fun. I'd probably enjoy being a Girl Scout these days. They might even let me put up the flag.

How We See Ourselves

I was talking to my mother on the phone the other day. She's eighty-six. "When are the kids leaving on their trip?" she asked me during the conversation.

"The kids?" I said. "Who do you mean?" She was talking about my sister and her husband. They're almost sixty, but Mama still thinks of them as "the kids." And of course, I still think of her as Mama, the same thing I called her when I was a child. The way we see ourselves might not be the same way others see us.

Lunching with a group of mature women in a restaurant, a friend who is a novelist said that she had heard a fortyish publicist speak about promoting oneself. The publicist suggested that we should try to find something different or unusual about ourself and accent that.

"One woman," the publicist had said, "was sixty-five years old, so we made a point of that. We scheduled her for appearances all over North Carolina. And do you know, she drove *herself* all over the state?"

The laughter at our lunch table pealed so loudly and for so long that heads turned at other tables. Sixty-five-year-olds apparently see themselves as capable of doing the same things that forty-year-olds do—in spite of how younger people view them.

There are a lot of us older adults out here, and it seems that soon society might begin to acknowledge not only our presence, but our physical vigor—as well as our spending power—at midlife.

I read that there are more than seventeen million American women who are fifty-five or older. And many of them endure clothing that's too tight here or too loose there. Sizing today is based on measurements that were taken in the 1940s. Most of the women used for those measurements were in the Army and only 2 percent were over fifty. Ten thousand women are now being measured to develop better-fitting clothing for women in the older-than-fifty-five age group. At last, merchandisers are seeing older women as paying customers with their own needs. Midlife consumers want to wear well-fitting and stylish clothes just as young people do.

Vanity never dies. But one day, we glimpse ourselves passing a shop window. At first, it seems someone else is wearing our dress, but then we realize it's us, and we don't look like teenagers anymore.

Our physical appearance changes, and we change our makeup, hair color, and hairstyle. We don't wear sleeveless dresses anymore; diet and exercise can do only so much. We sometimes choose plastic surgery to maintain the image we have of ourselves, wanting to look as good as we feel.

But we change in other ways too, more subtle, maybe more important ways. We begin to mellow, to be a little easier on ourselves. A poet friend of mine said on her fiftieth birthday, "I'm satisfied with what I've done—and with letting go of the undone."

I think that's important. To be satisfied with most of what we've done and been in life, and to be willing to let go of other things we may not have completed or which may never have worked out—and to let go without guilt or apologies—shows that we are mature adults. We stop ricocheting off the walls, trying to be everything to everybody. It's easier said than done, of course.

We continue to see ourselves as the only providers of all comforts for our children, now in their thirties themselves. I still worry about whether my children are warm enough, for heaven's sake, even though they've had their own homes for years. Gifts tend to take the form of flannel shirts, soft bathrobes, or down comforters. It's hard to let go of old instincts. Once a mom, always a mom.

But I did manage to let go in another way not long ago. I was recently in California to help my mother prepare for major surgery. Even though I love Florida, I've always pined for California, where I used to live. This time, I drove around a lot, researching nursing homes and doing errands. I was in and out of the grocery store and gas station and post office. I was virtually living in California for a period of time, not just visiting. And I realized California is not magical.

I already live in a good place. I like my neighborhood, my activities, my friends. California has traffic lights and fast-food restaurants and urban decay as well as blue skies and palm trees, just as we have in Florida.

I stopped yearning to be somewhere else. I realized I'm already home—and after all these years I've settled down. I let go of the undone (moving back to California) without regrets, and I feel much more centered. That's the kind of thing I think my friend meant.

There are many parts to our self-image. We see ourselves as being strong, healthy, and self-confident; as consumers, workers, parents, and caretakers; as being as vain as the next guy; and also as chronic American transients, still lighting out for the territories. All things considered, our composite self-image at midlife is realizing that we are—finally and unequivocally—the official national Grown-Ups.

Cars

The driver's license has long been the symbol of coming of age. It represents mobility, freedom, independence, and escape from parental eyes. At sixteen, we are recognized by the state as being grown-up, whether we are or not. Inversely, one of the most difficult stages of life is giving up the driver's license, along with our independence and mobility, when we are too old to drive. The license also serves as a proof of identity, and so it becomes, along with the passport, one of the most important documents in our lives.

Because the automobile represents adulthood, our cars become symbols of our self-worth. Men, more often than women, seem to feel that they *are* their car. If he has a good car, he is a good man. Most people would like to have a good-looking vehicle, but women tend to see cars mainly as transportation. Although some women care a great deal about appearance and style in automobiles, a lot of women don't care if the bumper is dented, if the car is red or blue, or if it was washed recently. They want the thing to turn on and go. There is nothing as useless or frustrating as a car that won't run, no matter how classy it looks.

The lack of female interest in cars was demonstrated in 1956 when, according to the *Los Angeles Times,* an auto manufacturer courted the woman buyer with a vehicle called La Femme. The car was available only in pink and lavender, and included matching purse, umbrella, raincoat, and boots. To the sellers' surprise, women were able to resist pastels. Only one thousand customers were willing to pay for cute in cars.

Men, however, find an ego satisfaction that goes far beyond the practical uses of an automobile. They take pride in flexing their muscles in the company of a car. Men call their cars "she" and "her" and refer to them as being "hot." "She handles like a dream," they'll say.

Long legged, beautiful young women are often pictured squirming on the hoods of cars offered for sale. This might mean beautiful women are attracted to small, red things, or it might mean you will meet a beautiful woman if you buy that car.

Car salesmen are beginning to take women shoppers seriously now. The last time I bought a car, the salesman spoke to me voluntarily without my having to search him out; he spoke earnestly as if he thought I might buy a car from him and did not ask if my husband were going to be joining me.

It is prudent to be polite to women customers. Recent reports say that on average, 55 percent of the people who buy cars are women. Even more women have an influence on which car is bought for the family.

I'd be frustrated without the independence of being able to get in my car and go where I need, or just want, to go. I do not look forward to the day when I'll have to give up my driver's license. It's one of those realities at the back of one's mind that we think always happens to someone else, not to us.

It's the Journey That Counts

"How was your trip?" friends ask. Depending on how recently I've returned, I might or might not give a gracious response. Yesterday, the first day following a two-week odyssey, I could not remember my phone number, the combination to my bicycle lock, or how to turn on my computer. This is called PTA: Post Trip Amnesia. It generally lasts two or three days.

My friend, Marie, says that when she gets back from a trip, she just wants to plant her feet firmly on the ceiling and stay there for a week.

Airline travel is especially exasperating. I feel like a dog. People tell me to sit . . . and stay. They feed me when it is convenient for *them*. Sometimes the food resembles table scraps.

Among the crowd at the airline terminal the other day was a couple who were probably in their fifties or sixties, each with a bulging shoulder bag. The man said, "It's okay to smoke in that section," and started off for the indicated area. The woman stopped still in her tracks.

"I need food," she said. She had to say it again, loudly, before the man heard her and saw that she wasn't following him. He then seemed to realize that she, too, had needs, appetites, wants. They changed direction, heading toward the snack bar.

It reminded me of how traveling used to be. We were much more likely to go by car than by plane in the 1950s. Getting into the car to leave for summer vacation, women never knew when they'd get out again. Husbands never got hungry, never got thirsty, never got tired, and never had to go to the bathroom.

Thank goodness cars are mechanical. The only time we stopped was when the car ran out of gas. Stopping at the gas station was our chance to get out, freshen up, forage for junk food, and try to get the blood recirculating through our legs before continuing the endurance test.

The destination used to be the point of going on a trip. We'd be hell-bent to get to the city, the campground, the motel we'd assigned ourselves as the goal for that day. There was often talk of getting an early start, like 4:30 A.M.

We were all June Cleavers and tried not to complain. We were on vacation, weren't we? We were having fun, weren't we?

Our parents called coping during the Great Depression the "art of hoping." Traveling with a man was an exercise in hope, too. "We'll stop in the next town," he'd say as the car passed two Gas and Good Eats establishments—and also the next town.

Things are better now that we're older. Old guys are easier to travel with. They have to go to the bathroom more often than they used to.

And somewhere along the way, women finally stopped being seen and not heard. When we began to allow ourselves to talk, we learned that husbands were not mind readers.

"I didn't know you wanted to stop," he said. "Why didn't you say so?"

To our surprise, we found that he had no idea that we were uncomfortable, hungry, or seething with resentment. So we've learned to talk and they've learned to listen better than we did when we were thirty.

Now, we don't even have a firm itinerary. If traveling by air, we might make a motel reservation for the first night, then rent a car and wing it, taking back roads to see where they lead us, stopping to listen to the silence of the wilderness of Arizona, deciding to skip the Grand Canyon and go on to Zion.

We even have enough self-confidence by this time of our lives to take separate vacations, each following his or her interest. Group tours make this easy. People with different interests have a lot more to talk about. Although it's fun to share a trip with your Best Friend, after seeing and doing the same things together all day, there is little news to report over dinner.

So now that we're giving ourselves choices ("I need food!"), we can also relax and enjoy ourselves and each other along the way. By the time we've traveled this far through life, we've learned that it's the journey and not the destination that counts.

Airline Travel

Traveling used to be a social event. In the 1960s, we'd get all dressed up in our beige dresses and circle pins. Our hair was beehived and sprayed so stiffly that it wouldn't have ruffled if the plane blew up and we fell twenty thousand feet to the ground. We would have hit the ground with our hair perfect.

Today, they let anybody on airplanes—even hitchhikers traveling space-available in their ultracasual cutoffs with overhead luggage that came from the grocery store checkout counter. (Paper or plastic?)

In those days the stewardesses, as they were called, were all young and pretty. Today, flight attendants come in assorted ages and sexes and look like real people.

I used to complain that regardless of whether I sat on the aisle, next to the window, or in the middle seat, the stewardesses would flutter over the male passengers next to me. Only after the men had their coffee, tea, or milk would the stewardess look at me, probably without even speaking, to see what I wanted. Now they serve either from aisle to window or vice versa. They don't try to serve men first, and the simpering silliness has changed for the most part to simple courtesy.

But old habits die hard. I often take care of the tickets. I think my husband feels out of control when we fly because someone else is driving. The last time we traveled together, I presented the tickets at the check-in desk and answered the questions about luggage and seat placement. Then the agent reached across me and handed the tickets to my husband, who was standing to the side. Smiling brilliantly, she told him what gate to look for. I stood there with my hand out and my mouth open.

Other things have changed on airplanes. For one, the seats are smaller. Either that, or I'm bigger. There are in-flight movies, and there are even air-to-ground telephones. Airline food is changing. Instead of hot meals, sandwiches are often served. It's a great improvement. It's hard to ruin a sandwich. Breakfasts have changed from omelets to cereal. Not long ago, we ate cereal at home before we left early in the morning, were served cereal again on board, and again after changing planes in Dallas. By that time, we were ready for lunch, but the time kept changing, and it was still morning in America.

For three years we were a military family. When my husband was in the navy, we accompanied him to the Philippine Islands for a three-year tour of duty. Our children were three and six.

That was the period of time when *we* were the hitchhikers. We could fly free on military aircraft when space was available. More then once we got up at 4 A.M. in Subic Bay in the Philippines and drove to Clark Airbase. We'd stand in line for a couple of hours and then, about 8 A.M., find out there was no space for us. We'd trudge back to Subic and unpack our bags.

One time, we did fly to Bangkok and then to New Delhi. It was on a troop transport plane, and the seats faced backward. We were told it was safer than facing forward. There weren't any windows. A lunch of Swanson TV dinners was served, but not until 3 P.M. At least the price was right.

It's no fun to travel if you can't complain, so now we complain about little things—like the way the flight announcers always, *always* say that we will be taking off "momentarily." Yeah? And then what? We're going to take off for a moment and then come right down again? Crash at the end of the runway? I want to get off now. Oh, well. I'm easily entertained.

And we complain that the seats were bigger in 1960. I know they were.

Names

I was married on the same day Jacqueline Bouvier married John Kennedy. Neither of us kept our maiden name as our surname. I don't know about her, but it never occurred to me that it might be possible, or even desirable, to keep my family name. In fact, at the time, I would have thought it illegal. In retrospect, it was probably custom, not law.

Even Hillary Rodham conformed to custom by taking her husband's name. Immediately after his inauguration, however, she began using her family name in conjunction with her married name. A little wordy for journalists, Hillary Rodham Clinton, but at least she made her point. It's her name.

Today, people are allowed to make choices about their last names. Women keep their maiden name, take their husband's name, use both and hyphenate them, or take a brand new name. For instance, if Bergdorf marries Olsen, they can combine the names and become the Bergsens. Legally, you can take any name you want to, as long as you don't use it to commit fraud. There is a lot of nonsense about pyramiding hyphenated names until children have eight last names, but I don't think that's a realistic concern. Choices will be made when necessary.

And choice is what it's all about. But having the freedom to choose is threatening to some people. Listen to this true story. (The names have been changed, however!)

They were not a young couple. Both had been married before. They were in love. He had two children. The children adored her. The invitations were ordered, and the church reserved.

"Because," she said, "my name is Wilson and yours is Plotzelheimer, why don't we use my name as our married name? It would be easier. At least we wouldn't have to spell it out all the time."

He was so alarmed by this suggestion that he broke the engagement. He gave up a woman he loved and a mother for his children as well as her additional professional income.

She wasn't even sure she wanted to make her name the family name. She just wanted to talk about it. After observing his reaction to her suggestion, she decided she was well out of an unhealthy situation.

A lot of women use their married name socially, but use their maiden name—or the name of their first husband, if they have become known in their own right by that name—for business. I know one sophisticated and talented middle-aged woman who has a short, simple last name. Her artist husband has a complicated surname. When they travel, they often use her name for hotel reservations and the like. Her husband doesn't feel threatened by this efficiency.

Taking the matronymic as the family name isn't a new idea. Una Stannard writes in *Mrs. Man,* her book about women's names, of the National Woman Suffrage Association's 1880 resolution stating: "That since man has everywhere committed to woman the custody and ownership of the child born out of wedlock, and has required it to bear its mother's name, he should recognize woman's right as a mother to the custody of the child born in marriage, and permit it to bear her name."

Women, after all, take most of the responsibility for children, bearing them and caring for them. In a single-parent home, the parent is most often the mother. So why not take the mother's name for the family name?

In the eleventh century, people in Europe did not yet have last names, but almost everyone did by the fifteenth century. The names represented the work people did (Mason, Carpenter), where they came from (West, Rivers), or who their family was (Johnson).

Stannard explains that until the 1870s, people thought that the life force for impregnation came from the father. Therefore, the child was named for the father. Then scientists learned that the ovum also contributes life and characteristics. A man sometimes took the matronymic if it was the only way he could receive a title or an inheritance from his mother. Even in colonial times, women almost universally used their own *first* names. It was Betsy Ross, not Mrs. John Ross.

The freedom to choose a surname is an idea that has taken hold in a very short period of time—just one generation. At my age, I take my husband's surname for granted, but I think it is a change for the better that people of both genders now have a choice.

Changing a name in the 1990s is a test of paperwork survival skills. In addition to changing the driver's license, there are voter registration, passport, charge cards, bank accounts, insurance forms, library card, Social Security papers, and on and on. If for no other reason than convenience, I think women are right to keep one name all through life—just as men have always done.

Bad Hair Day

We've always had Bad Hair Days, they just didn't have a name. The first time I heard the expression, I knew exactly what it meant. When your hair looks bad, everything else will go bad too. Bleach will spill on your favorite black blouse, the car won't start, and checks will bounce. Bad Hair Days are real.

The hair adjustment fetish has been with us all of our lives. Even as children, we put up with torture to make our hair look good. Our mothers introduced us to permanent waves. We squirmed under those dome-shaped things with electric jellyfish tentacles clamped to rollers on our heads. The heat was enough to fry our eyeballs, but we tolerated it. We came out with frizzy hair, not waves. After one go-around with this when I was too young to know any better, I cried for three days about the frizz.

And don't forget the Toni home permanents. The stench of ammonia would linger in the house for hours. My father never got done complaining about the inconvenience of living with women. I was in high school before I refused permanents and then found out my hair was naturally wavy. My mother had been trying to "fix" me for so long, I didn't know what my hair was really like.

No matter how much we learn about feminism, women still think they need repairs. Only the techniques and salons have changed. The salons are much more glamorous now. They used to be called beauty shops and looked like kitchens with linoleum on the floor. The stations were separated, each one enclosed in a private booth, as if what we did there was shameful. Today, shops are open and elegant. The ammonia, however, remains.

Men are beginning to come around to Bad Hair Days. Now they, too, need conditioners, hair spray, and permanents. They let their hair grow long and wear pony tails. Some men think baldness is a Bad Hair Day while others consider it sexy. Men know how to turn a disadvantage into an advantage. But women still are the principal hair-correction consumers.

One of the traditions of beauty salons is the "Isn't it gorgeous?" phenomenon. Usually I don't indulge in much more than a regular cut, but every couple of years, I forget about the pain of having my hair frosted. It's like labor, you forget it when it's over. It's the price of looking like a California girl. A rubber cap peppered with tiny holes is pressed over the entire head. Then the hair is pulled through the little holes with a crochet hook. It hurts a lot. A friend of mine takes aspirin before she goes for this abuse. Or codeine if she can get it.

Recently, however, I decided I should change the color completely. I said I wanted pale, platinum hair. "Not yellow," I said. "I can't wear yellow."

As I sat under the dryer, my hairdresser, Claire, whom I trust completely with the scissors, wandered by from time to time and pulled out a strand of my hair, fingered it, and then, without commenting, went back to drinking coffee. Then another hairdresser walked by and said, "Oh, it's going to be *gorgeous!*" Immediately, I was on guard. She couldn't even see my hair under the dryer. They teach them to do this in hairdresser school.

Eventually, I was moved to the chair for styling, with my back to the mirror so I couldn't see what was going on. At least two other workers who had always ignored me with great hauteur came by to say, "It looks *great!*" "Wow, what a terrific color! You're going to love it." They drifted around like schools of barracuda.

Finally, I'm turned around to face the mirror.

"It's *orange,*" I holler.

"Maybe it's a little warm," is the soothing verdict. "It's just the light in here. Let's go outside in the natural light." We go out to the parking lot with a hand mirror.

"It's *orange,*" I say. My skin has turned grey-green.

Back inside, the aesthetician is consulted. She lifts and drops strands of hair, but doesn't speak to me. Instead, she talks over my head to Claire. Information is transferred in code, such as, "Did you try P10? Maybe Ash 18. What color are her eyes?"

"They're blue and yellow," I say, training them on her full strength. A knowing glance is passed over my head.

"Ash 18," the consultant says.

An hour and a half later, I leave with a pressure can of color to take home for further rehabilitation.

After several months of haircuts and repeated applications of Ash 18, I begin to feel that my hair is less warm. Some days, I don't think about my hair for hours at a time.

My son comes to visit. He is the type who is unaware of physical beauty and appreciates people for their inherent worth. He wouldn't notice if you had your clothes on or not.

After a welcoming hug, he says, "Ma, why is your hair orange?"

Shoes

I am tormented by those pretty young women who work in bank buildings and attorneys' offices. They are still flirting their skirts and running their little feet in short tapping steps at 4:30 in the afternoon when I *know* they have been wearing those high heels all day long. They aren't even whining or limping.

It doesn't make any difference how many pairs of shoes I have or how sensible they are. There is just no such thing as the right pair of shoes. I always think the next pair will be perfect. If I could just have the sandals with the pink and purple straps, it would almost be like going barefoot, and my feet would be content at last.

Sometimes I think the proper functioning of the whole world is based on the game plan that shoes fit everyone comfortably. All jobs except lifeguard are assumed to be possible while simultaneously wearing shoes. We are expected to wear shoes when leaving our home and to go about our business during the day without complaining and without ostentatious or pitiful limping.

Even when shoes are reasonably comfortable, any pair will become annoying after a few hours. There is nothing like the toe-wiggling pleasure of being barefooted. I tend to remove my shoes—even sandals—whenever possible. Going barefoot is the first choice for comfort. This, however, is not always practical.

Shoe Rules are governed by buildings. It is not acceptable to go into a public building without shoes. This is dictated and controlled in part by stares from the Ladies who Lunch and partly by signs: No Dogs, No

Drinks; No Shirt, No Shoes, No Service.

I have too many pairs of shoes. Not as many as Imelda Marcos, but maybe she felt the same way I do. Maybe she also thought, "The next pair, the ones with the pink and purple straps . . ."

Front Flies and Other Impedimenta, or, What Do Women Want?

Every time I go shopping for jeans or a pair of slacks, I find that most of them have a front fly. I don't need a front fly.

Front plackets make me look fat. The extra folds of fabric plus a zipper in front are lumpy. A back or side zipper doesn't add to my already adequate girth.

Front flies started with Rosie the Riveter in the Second World War. The men went to war, and the women went to work in the defense factories. There were no women's work clothes then, so Rosie wore what was available—men's overalls and shirts and pants.

World War II has been over for some time now. We don't even have ration stamps for sugar and butter anymore. But the clothing manufacturers have kept on with the front flies as though we were still in mortal conflict. Now they even put front flies on skirts.

Then there is the alteration altercation. When I go shopping with my husband, I see that men's pants on the rack aren't hemmed. That's because the department store people plan to hem the pants at the right length for their customers. If he buys a sport coat, they will make that fit nicely too. *Free.* After he chooses what he wants, the tailor comes trotting out. Everyone is all smiles, little chalk marks are made here and there, and the clothes are whisked away. When the new duds come home, they look as if they belong to him. They fit him comfortably. He doesn't have to roll the pants legs up, as I often do, pretending the grunge look is in.

I do not sew well, or even cheerfully. Instead, I take my purchases to an alterations shop and pay to have them corrected. Some women's shops will do alterations at no charge, but it is not common in department stores. After being sued a few years ago, Saks Fifth Avenue in New York did agree to eliminate charges for *some* alterations on women's clothes.

I bought a suit at a well-known men's clothing store that also carries women's clothes. Their clothing is of good quality, and they charge appropriately. My jacket was altered through the shoulders and the sleeves were shortened. There was no charge for this. But the skirt needed to be shortened. I was charged eight dollars. I wrote to the president of the company complaining of the skirt tax. He responded by saying that because the skirt had to be taken apart and was not left unhemmed as men's pants are, there had to be a charge for it. (The fact that the jacket alteration required taking the sleeves apart, as well as the lining, and moving the buttons was apparently not a problem and did not require an extra fee.) I received an apology and my eight dollars were refunded.

Men's shirts come in both neck sizes and sleeve lengths. Women's shirts come in sizes four to sixteen. I have never in my life bought a long-sleeved shirt that had sleeves the same length as my arms. We pay the same price for clothes as men, but ours don't fit. Men's shirts are usually made better. The seams are stitched down and lie nicely flat. Even when I pay more for a blouse, I have to press the inside front to make it lie neatly. Sometimes I buy men's shirts even though they are too big for me because they are made of good material and are well constructed. And they're often cheaper.

Someone once said "If women are so smart, how come they have blouses that button down the back?" Good point. I used to think a valid reason for getting married was to have someone to do the back buttons. At least we have plenty of blouses that button up the front now, just like real people.

More good news: Now that auto manufacturers know women buy and drive cars, they plan to make cars comfortable for their customers. They are putting nets in the trunk to keep the groceries from falling down. Wow.

Talk of makeup kits in the dashboard and pink steering wheels, however, was not well received. Women keep their makeup in their purses, not in the car. And what is this pink fetish? Hoteliers also had a thing with pink for a while. They thought it was businesswomen's favorite color. They painted hotel rooms pink but put no skirt hangers in the closets. But they're getting better. They've learned women will be able to sleep even with off-white walls, and almost all hotels now have at least a couple of skirt hangers.

What do women want? The same thing other people want. Stuff that works for them.

In Praise of Older Women

In all your amours you should prefer old women to younger ones . . . because they have greater knowledge of the world.
—Benjamin Franklin

And what do older women prefer? Younger men, apparently. I thought these liaisons were not common, but when I began asking, they showered around me like oak leaves in a wind.

When I talked to older women who were involved with younger men, I learned that although hot, steamy sex was definitely a factor, it was third on their list. Communication and caring came first. Young men offer all three.

Older women found young men easier to talk to than men their own age. A lot of older men still consider women's conversation trivial. In social situations, they seem to prefer talking shop with each other. Wives complain they don't talk at all.

Young men, raised in the more open 1960s, are more likely to talk to women of any age, and are more likely to take an interest in what women are doing, thinking, feeling. Young men tend to be more open about their own activities and feelings, too.

Here are some love stories.

Diane lived with Michael for more than a year. He was twenty-four at the time. She was fifty-two.

Michael was a friend of Diane's daughter and often came to visit with other young college people. Diane, who was married to an alcoholic, had gone back to college and would be at the kitchen table studying while the young people were having fun in the living room. But Michael would spend the whole evening in the kitchen, talking to her—

spirited literary conversations about school work and ideas. He helped her edit her term papers.

They graduated the same year. Diane had a celebration party, and Michael was included. She wore a pretty dress with a center slit to the knees. Proud of her newly-earned college degree, she was having fun, sitting on the kitchen counter after a glass or two of champagne, kicking her foot as she talked to her guests. Her shoe fell. Michael knelt at her feet and replaced the shoe.

"As he put the shoe on my foot," she said, "he looked up at me, and at that moment I could see in his eyes that he was in love with me. And I knew then that I was in love with him, too."

But it was another year before they acknowledged their mutual attraction. After Diane left her husband, she and Michael lived together for about eighteen months. Then Michael left to go to graduate school on the West Coast.

"In many ways," Diane says, "he was more mature than I. It was he who would take my hands and talk to me and help me calm down when I was upset. If we quarreled, he would say, 'Don't turn away. We can talk about it.' I could never talk to my former husband that way."

Carl, forty-five, is seriously involved with Janet, who is fifty-four. "Not a great deal of difference," I said. "You are the same generation."

"It's a lot," he said. "When I was a high school freshman, I would never even have dated a senior. But now my sister is married to a man ten years younger, too.

"I wasn't looking for a younger woman," Carl said.

He was in the process of divorcing his first wife before he started dating Janet. It took him a while to convince Janet that his invitations were serious. She even offered to arrange a date with a friend closer to his age.

"I didn't want someone the age of a daughter, someone I'd have to take care of," Carl said. "Janet is mature and has a sense of humor. She's someone I can discuss things with and has a good head on her shoulders. She dresses well and looks better than some younger women. And she keeps herself in good condition—she can keep up with me, jogging. My first wife, who was three years younger than I, never could do that. I have a lot of respect for Janet. She's a real class act."

Another woman dated a younger man for a long time, thinking there were five or six years difference in their ages. At her fortieth birthday, she told him her age and was appalled to learn that there were eleven years between them.

He was not concerned about the age difference.

"Listen," he said, "I've been to Greece, and you haven't; you've been to forty, and I haven't. But someday, you'll get to Greece, and I'll get to forty. In the meantime, let's talk about something else."

Regrets

RSVP regrets only is a familiar notation in the lower-left corner of an invitation. If responding with regrets—not about party attendance—but about our lives, what would we list? That trip to France? Certainly. Always a mistake. Never having owned a Harley? Maybe allowing too many people to be houseguests for too long, or most important, not eating enough barbecued ribs.

Janet Landman has written a book called *Regret: The Persistence of the Possible* which might be the definitive work on the subject and is possibly more than you and I need to know about it. An excellent tome, nevertheless, it addresses the intricacies of regret in detail. Landman writes that lack of education is the regret mentioned most often, followed by affairs of the heart, and work. She also notes that the past is not so much discovered as it is constructed.

I don't have a lot of regrets. For instance, I would have married the same man and had the same education, although I've always wondered what it would have been like to go to school somewhere grand like Wellesley.

I regret not having long, slim legs. Everyone knows that if you have long, slim legs, you don't need anything else. For years, I thought if I could swim often enough and far enough, my legs would get longer, but they never did. Ballet might have helped.

I read of writers twenty, thirty years younger than I. *They* have seventeen books published. I'm jealous, envious, angry, and sulky. It's not fair. If only I'd gone to Wellesley.

If I had it to do over, I would have:

♦ Ridden on more roller coasters more often.
♦ Looked like Veronica Lake and been a famous movie star.
♦ Taken the gold for swimming the butterfly in the Olympics. (Fat chance.)
♦ Refused to be interrupted by people taller than I.
♦ Smacked the next person who used *hopefully* incorrectly. I don't care if William Safire is willing to allow it. I'm not.
♦ Learned to fly an airplane.
♦ Been able to remember at least 50 percent of everything I read: titles, authors, and all.
♦ Grown up before my kids did.

Just Say No

A friend once called and asked me to pour tea for a charity fashion show—the last thing I'd be caught doing. I said, "I don't do that sort of thing." I guess she was inspired by my refusal because she told me years later that she resigned from three organizations after that conversation. It is still one of her favorite anecdotes.

We fifty- and sixty-year-olds are often freelancers working at home. Sometimes this takes the form of retirement. (I'm not retired. I have two part time jobs: writing and moonlighting as a homemaker. Elaine Fantle Shimberg says homemaking pays better, but the writing is my essence.) This doesn't mean we have unlimited time to do everything that everyone else wants us to do. We still have our own lives to live, and after fifty we feel we have earned the right to decide how we spend our time.

Our friends eagerly evangelize to convince us their pet interest is important, and we should join them. But not everyone is interested in the same activities. And sometimes we think that we must accept others' invitations to get involved just because they sound like compliments.

When you are asked to do something that you don't want to do, don't apologize to excess and don't explain. "I'm sorry, I won't be able to help you with that," will do it. If you try to explain, you'll likely get a lot of whining and reasons why you *can* or *should* do it. Be warned there might be a lengthy silence following your refusal, but hang in there. Most people cannot bear a void and will change the conversation.

When extraneous activities get in our way, interfering with our own special interests, we're exasperated. Why did I agree to go to lunch on Thursday? Why did I say I'd help with the bazaar? Why did I join a service club and say I'd be secretary and treasurer? All of these things sounded like a good idea at the time, but rest assured they will all bloom on the same day. Then we find ourselves running in circles but accomplishing little. We begin to think that life is "full of sound and fury, signifying nothing."

If we haven't learned to say no by the time we're in our fifties, we're probably living highly fragmented lives. I fluctuate between saying yes to everything that crosses my line of vision and following T.S. Eliot's advice to "Resign, resign, resign." I'm currently in a resign mode simply because I've overextended myself again.

Pruning from time to time is healthful. At first it seems radical, but new growth follows, often in better form. When we get rid of excesses, it helps us focus our attention on the things that we really want to do. After all, we don't live forever.

The first organization I resigned from was the Girl Scouts when I was ten years old. Not long after that, I resigned from piano lessons without seeking parental guidance. I was too wily to risk the response. So you see, I have good solid credentials for resigning and saying no. I give myself permission to make choices, but if those choices are no longer valid after a period of time, or if I've simply made a mistake, I give myself permission to change my mind.

Most of us have at least one altruistic activity that we cherish and don't want to give up. Doing a good job of a few things is more productive than paying lip service to many. Nowhere is it written that we must be Superfiftysomethings.

Swimming at Dawn

I don't know why I do this to myself. I don't know why I come, at dawn, still warm from my bed, and slide into a pool of deep water. My hair is sticking out, I have on no makeup, my nylon suit hides none of my secrets, and whatever critics I have are on hand to see me at my worst. And I them.

Have we no pride? While we swim long and hard, others stay in their beds. They shower and dress in the comfort and privacy of their own homes, brush and preen themselves, and prepare for a dignified assault on the day. Swimmers are bedraggled before the day even begins, dress in an echoing communal dressing room with only one outlet for the hair dryer, and have no privacy at all.

But I come again the next day, and as I sit on the edge of the pool and struggle my goggles into place, I become aware of sensual pleasures even before I am fully awake. Soon the flow of the water moves down my body, and I experience the exhilaration of stimulated circulation, a brightening of mood, a feeling of physical well-being.

There is something mystical about swimming on a cold morning when mist rises from the water and mingles with the fog. I see the sun rise not just occasionally, but several days a week. After more than twenty years in Florida, I still never take the luxury of swimming in an outdoor pool in February for granted.

Some good friends take time to develop. Swimmers are a solitary lot, doing their thing mostly deaf, dumb, and blind, underwater. It takes a while for swimmers to get acquainted, but when we finally do, we find that we have known each other for a long time, many sunrises already.

Swimming early has something to do with postponement of responsibility, an avoidance of adulthood for an hour or so. It is a daily renaissance. By the time I start my work I have already completed one of my goals for the day. Every time I get into the pool, I win, because I come out feeling well, stronger, brighter, and ready.

Why do I do this to myself? Because I love it.

A Room of One's Own

Like other animals, humans are territorial and become more so after fifty. The older we get, the more we cherish our own comfortable chair, our own clutter. Our instinct to burrow in and define our boundaries becomes stronger. We want our own lair, our own hangout.

Virginia Woolf advocated having a room of one's own—a place for favorite things, a place to work, to think, or just to be. She also advocated having an income of your own, but you'll have to work that out for yourself.

Having a room of one's own didn't occur to us sooner because we didn't have an empty room, but one day that last child grew up and moved out, and suddenly there was space available.

Your spouse will be eyeing the vacated room also. Don't argue. Don't delay. Take action.

- First, check the closets and chest of the empty room. I found a cat in a dresser drawer and banana peels and potato chip bags under the bed. None of this surprised me.
- Move the furniture out, repaper the walls, and take the curtains down, but keep the venetian blinds. Bring in a two-seat couch that does not change into a bed (this is a place of your own, not a guest room) and whatever else you want—a desk, a woodworking bench, a loom, a typewriter or computer, fly-tying gear, or a needlepoint basket. Books.

Accessories might include the old bookrack you made in shop class, high school yearbooks, *The African Queen* poster, photos of people and places you like.

You can use your own discretion about keeping living things in your room. Recalcitrant writer Fran Lebowitz wants nothing alive in her space, neither plant nor animal. I rather like a plant or at least a dried arrangement. If you have live things, however, you will have to feed, water, prune, brush, deflea, or otherwise clean up after them.

♦ Do not bring in a television. This is a place to be happy, not a place to be abused. You are a nice person, and you deserve some tranquillity at this stage of your life. Looking at the news ("The horror! The horror!") or at Eddie Albert clicking his dentures as he advertises hearing aids is not soothing for people in their fifties and sixties.

A room of your own is not the place for the ironing board, either.

♦ Do not allow your friends to bring in root or other beers. They might get the idea that they are welcome in your room. Insist that they knock and wait for an invitation to enter. Do not offer casual conversation. Let them sit on the couch and state their business. Keep a serious mien while you have visitors in your room. This is not a club. You are not taking applications for new members.

♦ On the other hand, eat your own lunch there whenever you want to. Or just bring in frequent feedings, such as a bran muffin, a mug of coffee, an apple, or a whole raspberry coffee cake from the grocery store.

♦ You might, however, sponsor a cocktail party there once or twice a year. This should be a formal occasion and have time limits as any other party would. Five to five-thirty would be suitable. This might be a good time to reinstitute the more traditional cocktails such as the manhattan. Remember the manhattan? Or the Rob Roy? Margaritas are good for vacations, but kind of yuppie at home.

♦ Have a phone in your room so you can call your friends and talk and laugh a lot. But I warn you—and there is no way to avoid this danger—one day that phone might ring, and it will be your daughter saying she is getting a divorce and is coming with the baby to take up residence in her old room.

Halloween

A witch used to be a cackling old hag who contracted with the devil through her agent, a black cat, to sour the milk of the neighbor's cow. But nothing is as it was in the good old days. The contemporary witch is as likely to look like—and be—the girl next door as not. She might very well have a black cat, but the neighbors are more likely to have a Datsun than a cow.

The contemporary witch in America is often involved with ecology and the conservation of animal and other natural resources as well as with potions and charms. I talked on the phone to a witch named Arta. She is nearing fifty but has the voice of a young woman, soft and slow, with a pleasant smoky edge to it. Patient with my questions, she talked about modern witches and about Wicca, the religion. "Most witches consider themselves Wiccan," Arta said. "Four and five hundred years ago, the Wicca were teachers and healers—the sages."

According to Margot Adler, the word *wicca* is Old English, referring to wit or wisdom. Others say the word derives from Indo-European roots meaning to bend or to turn. A witch, then, would be a wise woman or man skilled in the craft of shaping, bending, and changing reality.

In the modern world, witchcraft—wicca—can be learned through correspondence courses. More than forty thousand students have begun the twelve-week course, but only a couple hundred have completed it.

Witches also have a computer network. The Pagan Allied Network (PAN) connects most covens. A local radio station has aired programs featuring witches. There are magazines for witches.

"Today," Arta said, "witches are concerned with protecting the planet itself—Mother Earth. Our rituals are concerned with the seasons of the earth and the phases of the moon, so we hold harvest festivals in the fall and planting festivals in the spring. During the shorter days of winter, we celebrate the Yule festival. It's focused on the sun that is dying and will be reborn. October 31, All Hallow E'en (November 1 is All Soul's Day), is a time we pay respects to those who have died and gone on this year. It's thought to be a time when the veil between the worlds is very thin. The people who have died can look back or step back in spirit and say good-bye one more time."

Witches often work with natural herbs. Some are workers in the healing arts. "We have quite a few witches who are registered nurses," Arta said.

But the word witch has had rather bad press. "I accept the name witch," Arta said, "and wear it gladly because it pays homage to many people who were unjustly killed. No apology has ever been offered for the Inquisition."

A coven—a group of witches—can be as few as two or as many as can fit into a room. Tradition calls for thirteen. Some covens are all male, some all female, but the great majority are mixed. They get together for rituals. Or for birthday parties or whatever.

"A coven is like a family," Arta said, "a family of choice rather than of blood. You must be initiated into a coven. My coven sets out to work magic—to cause change. We don't have anything to do with the devil. He belongs to the fundamentalists."

But how about all the old ideas that we have grown up with? For instance, can witches still the wind?

"Some witches do believe they can control the energies that control the world. This includes weather. I don't think a weatherman would pay much attention to their statements. But many witches can have rain—or a clear day—when they need one. Yes. It's a very strong belief in the community."

And black cats?

"Almost everyone I know has an animal. No, they don't use them to cast spells. I have a dog who tears up the house if I close him out of the circle. All I have to do is start setting out candles, and he wants to be there. He feels something there that he likes. My cat, however, won't have anything to do with it."

Arta invited me to a sabbat of witches on Halloween night. I envisioned a slight rise of ground under moonlight and a boiling cauldron of mice and newts and pumpkin shoots. No such luck. Would you believe the witches celebrate with a potluck supper after the religious ceremony?

The Ballad of the Red Earrings

I was at the supermarket the week before Thanksgiving, dodging the racks of home videos, when I came up against a rack of Christmas tree ornament earrings—red, green, silver, or gold balls. The globes were made to dangle from a pierced ear.

Just the thing, I thought. Cheap ($2.95), outrageously gaudy, and in very poor taste. Christmas needs some lightening up.

The holidays should be fun, but frequently turn out to be work. Women make it that way, not men. Men might go along with it, but they would never work that hard and that long for something that lasts only one day and earns no profit. Instead, it costs a bundle.

Christmas is like a wedding. We try to construct a medieval pageant out of an occasion that is essentially a religious ritual. Both are celebrations of an important event, but we have such high expectations that we are sure to be disappointed. We work harder and harder and spend money faster and faster, trying to build castles and fairy tales when what we need is a little silliness to enhance the festivities.

This comes from a celebrant who clearly remembers her third Christmas. Even then, I knew there was no Santa Claus and did not understand why the grown-ups were so crazy as to foster the idea. I also knew I'd better keep my little pink mouth shut or I might not get any presents. A babe swaddled in cynicism.

I didn't buy the silly earrings the day I bumped into them. For one thing, it wasn't even Thanksgiving yet, and for another, I'm stingy—except when it comes to books and shoes. It just seemed too soon to think about Christmas.

I used to be irritated by the store decorations, gift wraps, and bins of packaged perfumes that appear right after Thanksgiving. It seems we have holiday decorations so much of the year that I really don't pay attention to them anymore. This year, however, it was even earlier— before Halloween. This isn't annoying, it's frightening. It means that business and the economy must be bad, and merchants must try harder to make their profits, to earn their living.

I thought about the earrings after I got home and decided that the next time I was in the store, I'd buy them. The red ones, I decided. No, the silver. No, red.

You are expecting a great epiphany here—but there isn't one. The earrings did not change the world or me or anyone I know. No star rose in the east. I bought them (red) and put them on at the counter. Then I bobbled around the store, collecting canned pumpkin for the pie— remember this was before Thanksgiving—grapefruit, eggs, the usual. But I noticed that people were smiling at me. I don't think they were laughing at the earrings. It was fun wearing them and I was smiling first.

Easily entertained, you are thinking. Yes, that's true. It's this simple kind of thing that makes the season. It's being able to release the child within us, to be childlike and have some fun while we're working hard at the serious business of the holidays.

At my age, you have permission to be a little silly, to begin practicing to be eccentric—if you haven't become so already. Even a cynical matriarch like me.

Weight-Bearing Activity

I've been reading Betty Friedan's book, *The Fountain of Age*. Among other things, she writes of a wilderness adventure in which she shoots rapids, rappels cliffs, and is alone in the woods for twenty-four hours.

I don't even like to walk around the neighborhood for thirty minutes. Swimming is my game, but my doctor says I need thirty minutes, three times a week, of what she calls "weight-bearing activity."

Walking makes me keenly aware of my hip joints. I never used to know I had hip joints. Walking makes my hands swell. Maybe I should get some of those weights to carry. I sweat. My hair gets saturated and sticks out in crinkles. My muscles bunch up. So does my brain.

My sister walks four miles in about an hour. I don't know what distance I walk. I've established several routes that take half an hour: to the park and back, over the bridge and back, to Fourth Street and back.

I promise myself I will use the time to think, plan, meditate, become a better person. Instead, I stumble over uneven sidewalks, watch addresses to see how much farther I have to go, and look for cats. If I see five cats, it's a good omen, and I feel encouraged and brightened.

Cats, I notice, are too smart to take walks. They go about their cat business, sauntering as they check out their territory, tails overhead like flags on bicycles. They never exercise, though. After resting quietly all day, cats make a brief nocturnal foray or maybe sit on the front steps for a little while in the morning. So how come they look so svelte and I look so lumpy?

By the time I reach the farthest point of my itinerary, I've stopped thinking about my hip joints. I'm moving along a little more smoothly and beginning to see how the sunlight filters through the trees.

I make a planned effort to appreciate nature. In Florida, there are often trees in bloom: jacaranda, poinciana, magnolia. In the spring, the scent of jasmine and citrus is hypnotic and makes me feel dizzy, it is so wonderful. For two weeks in March, the silly azaleas riot and then become ordinary little green shrubs again until next year, their annual fifteen minutes of fame exhausted.

As I near the waterfront, I can see the water sparkling in the bay, the morning sun filtering lemon yellow rays through clouds and over the water. Elegant seagulls in white, grey, and black swoop and float on the air, harass each other, and laugh at me—earthbound, clumsy.

An early flight to Dallas drones over the bay. I've been on it, looking down at the same scene I'm traversing on foot now. In the park, I encounter beautiful young athletes, eyes straight ahead and skin glistening with their efforts. I try to pick up my pace a little, but don't adopt their all-out knockers-up stride.

There are gaggles of women walking together. They are all talking at the same time, wobbling along like a bunch of geese. They smile thinly as if they feel sorry for me, alone. Walking is miserable enough without inflicting half the neighborhood on yourself at the same time.

Finally, I turn my corner and come to my own street. It's all downhill now. I don't even check the house numbers, just head straight for home, comfort, food. In a last burst of energy, I take the key from my pocket, climb the steps to the porch, and unlock my front door. Inside, my big black cat looks up from the coffee table and yawns.

The hardest part of the day is over, I declare. Everything else will be easier. To recover from the self-abuse, I do twenty minutes of yoga, getting out the kinks and letting my mind come back to me. Now I can begin to think again. Even putting the early morning coffee cups in the sink seems a pleasure because I've done my weight-bearing activity, paid my dues for being over sixty, and now I can get a life.

Let Betty Friedan be a hero. I just want my Maypo.

Set in My Ways

I told my sister one day that I thought I was getting set in my ways, something about not wanting to change my routine. She, with her usual innate common sense, jerked me to attention.

"I'd like speak up for being set in your ways," she said. "What's wrong with routine? Sometimes there's comfort in doing things the same way. Goodness knows,we are bombarded with change all the time, and live in a world of impermanence and confusion. And how do we know change will be better, an improvement?"

We communicated these thoughts on our Prodigy programs. Prodigy represents a change in our communication methods that we had not foreseen even one year ago when we relied on a stodgy device known as the telephone. She has a copier, I have a shredder, but neither of us has a fax.

These changes in communication methods are fun. Other changes in our day-to-day world are not. We have voice mail, but find it impenetrable. Ibuprofen has replaced aspirin, but we have to add Metamucil to counteract the side effects, and we still can't get the tops off the bottles. Our glue-on fingernails get in the way.

Even in something as basic as language, changes are not always improvements and are often objectionable. The vulgar and obscene terms that are commonly used today are shocking. At least at first. After a while, they become just tedious and inane. In some movies, the infamous "f" word is used repetitively on every occasion when a verb, noun, or adjective is wanted.

Strong language is used so glibly that we no longer have a good cuss word. In high school, *hell* and *damn* used to be most satisfying, but now, if we are really mad and want to cuss, we don't have a suitable word left. They're all worn out and don't mean anything anymore.

I admit to being a slave to daily routine. I want the newspapers and mail sorted or discarded in the morning and the dishes in the sink before I can start work. Exercise needs to be out of the way early, too, or it won't be done at all.

I can get through breakfast without a list, but not much further. Some say this is too controlled, but I think it makes my life easier. In addition to a daily list, I make a short weekly list on Monday. Then I don't have to think about all the things I need to do in the coming week. Some things don't have to be considered until Friday. I can put those out of my mind until the proper day.

Being set in my ways, I still like to wear the same kinds of clothing that I have worn since 1940: skirts, pants, and shirts. I haven't changed to tights, miniskirts, or bustiers. A change that I do like in clothing is the variety of skirt lengths that are acceptable. We used to have to shorten or lengthen our hems every year or two, but now we can do whatever we like about that.

Repetition and routine can be comfortable, and, if it doesn't bother anyone else, I'll just continue to be set in my ways. Just leave me alone with my computer, my answering machine, my fuel-injected coupe, and a ready-made pizza in the freezer, and let me be an old fogy.

Am I Old Yet?

I don't know how we know when we're old. Maybe it's when we start ordering the Senior Citizen's Special at Denny's. The first time I did that, I expected to be carded but no, they took my word for it. That, I admit, caught my attention. And when I found out that I was an inch shorter than I was two years ago, I wondered if it were the beginning of the end.

I remember very well, however, when I knew that I was no longer a child. I was fifteen. It seems appropriate that I was in the kitchen when it happened—woman's place.

It was a summer morning about 9 A.M. I stood at the gas stove in the kitchen, frying bacon for my breakfast. The morning sun was streaming in the windows making shafts of motes, rosy and golden. There was an ethereal quality about the light—dappled, splashing about the narrow kitchen. My mother was nowhere around, which was unusual. She would usually be there warning me, "Be careful, don't spill, don't forget to . . ." It was also unusual that I was doing something just for myself: frying bacon.

I felt long-limbed and lean. I was wearing cutoff jeans and a plaid shirt, blues and greens. My clothes fit me. It was the first time I remember the sensation of clothing being just right. My clothes were bought large so I could "grow into them." I was growing fast enough that the clothes fit me before they were handed down to my sister. I felt like my self at that moment, not waiting to be myself at some future date. I seemed to be an entity.

I knew that that sunlit moment was fleeting, and then I emerged with the awareness that I would never be quite the same again, that I was moving forward in my journey. I was no longer a child but had advanced to the next stage of my life, whatever that would be. I was ready and luxuriated in that knowledge.

Knowing precisely when I became old, however, is not so clear. It is more of a mosaic with bits and pieces of awareness blending together into a whole. Many of those tiles of time were put into place in a kitchen. Many things are the same throughout. I wear my hair much as I did when I was fifteen: short, parted on the side. I still like to wear comfortable pants and buttoned shirts.

One image I have is of myself sitting at the table, again with the morning light coming in, and looking at the news on a small television set. A man was walking on the moon. I knew then that a line had been drawn, that that was an historical moment, and that I had become part of history. I knew that someday it would mark me: Old Enough to Have Seen the First Moon Walk.

Another day my son, grown and with his own home, complained to me about reading my comments in my newspaper column. "I used to have to listen to this stuff at home all the time, and now I have. *pay* for it," he said.

I laughed and laughed. It was a triumphant moment for me: sweet, sweet retribution. He could have listened to me in the first place—for nothing. I felt old and wise.

I also remember looking out the window and seeing my neighbor was moving out. She has been a good friend for many years. We had shared child rearing, husband rearing, social events, nude afternoon swims in her pool, going back to college, and finally—her divorce. She was moving to another state. It was the first time I shared this kind of pain with a friend. Others in my group divorced after that, but she was the closest, and I cried watching the transition take place. I felt older that day.

I've stopped trying to lose enough weight to look like a teenager, admitting finally that I am a mature woman with an appropriate body outline, and it actually feels good. A cartoon shows a square-bodied matron with her arms folded and a staunch look on her face. Built to Last, the caption reads. That's me.

I bought some of those shoes that look like the ones my mother used to wear—black wing-tip oxfords with chunky heels. They seem a great, witty joke, but they are still old woman shoes from the 1930s. "Crone shoes," my kids call them. "Yes!" I cry, shooting a fist into the air.

I enjoy being old more than I enjoyed being a teenager. I know who I am now, I'm more sure of myself and have more fun.

But even now, I'm not metamorphosed. I'm still learning and growing. Often, I feel like a butterfly still in her cocoon, the cocoon just beginning to open. I'm still struggling to get out, my wings trying to pull free and open, to fly in full color.

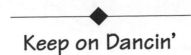

Keep on Dancin'

At a retirement party dinner table, a woman of my generation talked of a "sense of urgency."

"We've always lived in the future," she said, "We'll do this one day, or we'll take a trip to Australia next year. But the future is here. I'm in sort of a frenzy to do what I want to do before I die."

Others at the table agreed with her. We want to do the things we've talked about before we get too old, too feeble. We want to read, to travel, to learn, to experience those things which always seemed a goal to be considered at a later date. We postponed traveling until after the children grew up. After retirement, husbands would be able to relax and not get anxious after a week, wanting to get back to the office to see if everything was all right.

We think that someday, not right now but sometime soon, we'll learn Italian, rent an apartment in New York for three months and really get to know the city, finish that degree, reread all the books once loved or even just the new one on the bedside table.

Some of us are doing these things now and having a good time. Others cannot give up the occupations and habits of a lifetime.

Recently, when I was disappointed in a long-term project, I thought, *Maybe this is all I'm going to do in my lifetime. Maybe I should let go and quit struggling to accomplish more. Maybe this is it.* The old Peggy Lee song ran through my mind, "Is that all there is, my friend?"

The sense of time running out is not limited to people over sixty. A young friend said over lunch, "It suddenly occurred to me that maybe the little house we live in is going to be it. When we bought it, we thought that it would be fine to start with, and then we'd have something better when we could afford it. But now, I don't see that in the future. Our daughter is already fourteen and will be gone in a few years. Maybe we don't need more room." She seemed puzzled. This was not the future she had expected. But then, this was not yet "the future" for her, either.

At the other end of the spectrum, Louella and Harry, eighty-five and ninety-seven respectively, decided that the time had come to move into an assisted living facility. Now they feel that they did so too soon. They weren't old enough yet. They still feel that there are things to be done. They miss their swimming pool and more active friends. A trip to visit family is planned for this summer. Louella looks forward to the fall season when she will continue to play her cello in a concert orchestra.

No matter how old we get, we seem to have a sense of urgency. We never give up planning and hoping. Like Peggy Lee, we keep on dancin'.

The Old Glass Pitcher

Fifteen years ago, I bought a glass pitcher from an old St. Petersburg hotel called the Madison. The hotel was about to be razed to make room for what is now the parking lot of a bank. The hotel furnishings were being sold, and, for once, I heard about it before the sale was over.

I'm not an enthusiastic shopper and don't usually know what's going on. But this was a lucky day. For two dollars, I bought a sturdy one-quart glass pitcher, the kind that has vertical indentations, like a Greek column. I also bought a round glass tray. These two pieces have been in my kitchen for years now, the pitcher keeping water cold, the platter sometimes serving salads or birthday cake, or holding jars of coffee and rice and chili peppers.

But then one day, I tried to make iced tea in the pitcher and forgot to put a silver spoon in first, and so the pitcher cracked. It didn't break, but was now useless for holding fluids. I cried, which didn't make much sense. In fact, I was surprised that I felt so sentimental. Unlike a cherished old stoneware pitcher that had once held lemonade for my husband when he was a little boy, this was just an ordinary pitcher and had no family background. When we moved from the house we'd lived in for twenty years, I walked out and slammed the door without even looking back, but when my two-dollar pitcher cracked, I was desolate.

The pitcher was retired to the kitchen counter without any duties. Later, it was assigned to be the receptacle for cooking spoons next to the stove. The old pitcher is as comfortable and familiar as the handwriting of an old friend on an envelope.

When we shop for Christmas gifts, we want to find something that will be precious and loved for years, like the old glass water pitcher, but it's almost impossible to hit on just the right magic. And not even realistic to try. A friend rails against the injustice of having to shop for several gifts for everyone in the family. Each gift must be meaningful and personal, beautifully wrapped, and ready on the *same day*. Birthdays are bad enough, but the requirements of Christmas are an affront to rational adults.

The most casual gifts often become the most precious. One of my favorites is a shell filled with smaller shells that my husband collected for me one day on a beach in the Philippines. Another success is the little cigarette container that our son made in first grade for his father. His dad doesn't smoke anymore, but he still has the little ceramic pot on his desk, holding paper clips.

Sometimes we're hard pressed to find just the right thing. We are reduced to exchanging lists, which is simply a way of getting the things that we were going to buy anyway. The computer or dishwasher that we get for Christmas is exciting or necessary, but isn't the sort of thing that brings tears to the recipient's eyes.

The obvious gift often works well. It's impossible to have too many poinsettias. I think they are even more festive than Christmas trees, which look pallid as they dry out in the bright Florida sunlight streaming in the window.

One of my favorite gifts is a cow skull that I got for my birthday. It's chalk white, perfectly symmetrical, and is the last word in minimalism. It might not be your bag, but I love it and keep it in the living room as a sculpture. It has a definite Georgia O'Keeffe quality about it. It is especially valuable because it was found in the wilds of Brevard County, Florida. The donor had it in his living room, but, knowing I lusted for it, gave it up.

One year I gave my son—the donor of the cow skull—the Waterford sherry set that had belonged to his grandmother. It isn't a practical gift like Oxford-cloth button-down shirts, but he had always admired the set and was happy and touched to have it for his own.

I once admired a friend's Timex watch with Roman numerals. He wrapped it as a gift and gave it to me on my birthday. I still love to wear it, partly because I like the style and partly because it reminds me of my friend.

If you're down to the wire and want to give a surprise gift that wasn't on a list, you might look around your house for the sherry set, or maybe the nice old photo of Uncle Walt, or Grandma's pearl ring. Or yours. Or maybe you just happen to have an old pitcher—or an extra cow skull—lying around. Little things mean a lot.

Smokey, the Retired Cat

One of my earliest memories, when I was four years old, is searching the neighborhood with my mother, calling for my lost black kitten. A cat lover all my life, I've had as many as five cats at a time. Only for very brief periods have I had none. I remember one, Mary Anne, a tabby and a good mouser brought in from the SPCA for that purpose, who promptly presented me with (1) a dead mouse at breakfast and (2) five kittens which she then abandoned and left me to feed with an eyedropper. But she was the only cat who disappointed me.

When my son George was five, he helped Maria Elena, a black cat, deliver her kittens. He sat with her all day, even having his peanut butter sandwich lunch beside her basket. Eventually there was a surprised cry of "Something's coming out of Maria Elena, and it's got claws!"

Most of my cats have been neutered males. Recently, I was down to one. Due to attrition, Albondiga (Meatball) is a sixteen-year-old only-cat after being a member of a pride of five. He's what T.S. Eliot calls a Jellicle cat: black and white and rather small. He was one of those kittens that little girls give away outside supermarkets. Al and I have grown old together, and now we're both a little creaky when we get up in the morning.

At the veterinarian's office for my cat's annual checkup, I told Dr. Spears that Al seemed lonely.

A Cheshire smile crossed the doctor's face. He didn't hesitate for an instant. "Bring Smokey out here!" he called to his technician.

Dr. Spears got Smokey from a client who was moving to a place which did not allow pets. Smokey also had a urinary tract problem. The owner asked to have Smokey put to sleep.

The veterinarian asked if they could treat Smokey and then keep him as a hospital blood donor cat. "I explained that we'd take good care of him, and that when he got older, we'd find him a good home," Dr. Spears said.

Smokey had been the blood donor cat at the animal hospital for three years. He was now six years old. Dr. Spears said Smokey had saved hundreds of cats' lives. Smokey was living at the hospital, and, as nearly as I could tell, he was the boss there.

The doctor told me that six is retirement age for a blood donor cat. Smokey had done his share for the good of catkind and was ready to retire to a good home.

Smokey certainly didn't look debilitated. He was the biggest cat I'd ever seen. He weighed sixteen pounds, had a black coat of short, dense fur and serious gold eyes. To see him was to love him.

Animals have a special place in our lives. People grow old with their animals, and when it's time to move into a restrictive condominium or retirement home, it's hard to give them up. "It's even sadder when people go into nursing homes," Dr. Spears said.

At times we value our animal friends even more than some of our human friends. "I often tell people," Dr. Spears said, "horses, dogs, cats, whatever, have more of a bond to the human species than we do to each other sometimes. I've had pointer bird dogs all my life," he said. "I grew up with them. There are eight or ten that I've lost over the years, and it is *never* easy. You never replace that particular one. You get another one, but it's just never the same as old Jim was, or Jack. You still remember them for their own."

I was enchanted with Smokey as soon as I saw him, but having had cats all of my life, I knew the responsibility involved. I also knew that cats add elegance, a sense of humor, and comfort to my home. I admire their cynicism and their independence. I just like to look at them and touch them.

I wanted Smokey, but said I'd think about it. I wanted to consider the idea of taking an adult cat rather than a kitten. I know too well the pain of losing old friends, and Smokey is no spring chicken.

But, of course, after I got home, I couldn't think of anything else. Dr. Spears knew what he was doing. It was too late. I was already infatuated.

It took Smokey a while to get used to having more space and being outdoors again. But he has staked out his territory, done battle with the dreaded white cat down the street, and is a card-carrying alley cat again.

I can't understand why a black cat was named Smokey, which seems more suitable for a grey cat, but because he has brown mixed with his black, we sometimes call him Mocha as well as darling and love. But never, of course, do we call him late for dinner, as the saying goes. Little Al, at a puny eight pounds and with the wobbly back legs of an oldie cat, is still in charge, still the alpha cat. There was some hissing and booing when Smokey first came home, but that has diminished now. It must have been five months before Al allowed Smokey to come upstairs into the bedroom. On cold nights, however, they'll both be on the bed. A two-cat night is a cold night in Florida.

Someone to Wonder Where You Are

Some years seem to have more fires, floods, and earthquakes than others. Mother Nature does her thing and does it thoroughly, as if we need to be taught a lesson for our cantankerous human shortcomings such as war, violence, and general peevishness. She focuses our attention and makes us wonder about the essentials of life—not just the comforts, but the needs.

When disasters occur, we watch them on television as they take place, seeing people like us lose everything—returning home to find all they own is under four feet of water, or their house burned to rubble except for the fireplace. It makes us wonder, *What are my most precious belongings? What would I take if I had to leave home hurriedly?*

I remember a hurricane when we had to evacuate because of the danger of flooding. Before dawn, we moved to my husband's office where we remained for three days.

Like most people, I always thought that I would take my photo albums because they cannot be replaced. Maybe my favorite white shirt. Books! What about my books! Jewelry is the most easily transported and most valuable in terms of money, but that did not occur to me.

Instead, we put the throw rugs on the piano, left food and water, and opened the attic door for the cats to find higher ground if necessary; we forgot the photo albums and took something to read (Thomas Wolfe's six hundred-page *Look Homeward, Angel*—dry reading with an appropriate title). For some reason, we took sweaters, even though hurricane weather is not cold. That is a protective, mothering kind of instinct, keeping those you love warm and therefore safe from danger. And all weekend, we wished that someone had remembered the deodorant.

When we got home, the cats were sulky and some shrubs had been uprooted, but no real damage had been done. Somehow, the whole thing was kind of a lark, a charade.

We never think that disasters will happen to us, only to other people. I have no doubt that those who are closely involved in floods and fires take them more seriously. They are the ones who learn that there are some things we need and other things that are not essential.

My sister lives in Escondido, California, and was near the fires. She said it was amazing how resilient people were. One couple lost their home, clothing, and possessions of twenty-five years when the fires leveled their house. They said they had only lost material things, which meant nothing. They knew that others were worse off. In television interviews, people seem to feel that if they got out with their pets, they were lucky.

Disasters level homes and scatter belongings, but they also focus our priorities. Margaret Mead, anthropologist and one of our principal American crones, wisely commented on our human values. "One of the oldest of human needs is having someone to wonder where you are when you don't come home at night."

Letters

When sorting through the day's mail, the personal letter among the catalogs, bills, and overdue notices from the library rivets our attention instantly. We look at a personal letter the way we look at a lover—with eyes that see nothing else in the room. All attention is on the blue or ecru envelope, or even the plain white number ten, the envelope with handwriting instead of a computer-generated address sticker.

A personal letter is so delicious, the reading is postponed until coffee has been made, shoes removed, and feet propped on the coffee table. The letter must be opened with a letter opener, preferably an old and cherished one.

Letter writing is becoming a lost art, however. A common complaint in advice columns is the lack of even simple letters such as thank-you notes. Instead, we use telephones both at home and while driving our cars. Fax machines and computers are our written forms today. What will biographers use in the future if there is no paper trail?

Sujata Banerjee wrote that about 7 percent of our mail was personal correspondence in 1977. By 1989, it had dropped to 4.5 percent. It's probably less than that now.

Although midlife adults are more likely than younger people to write personal letters, we, too, have become addicted to the telephone. In 1940, we made long distance phone calls only in emergencies. "What's wrong?" our grandmothers would holler. We thought talking loudly was necessary because of the distance our voices had to travel.

Now we are able to make nonurgent long-distance phone calls

without feeling guilty—for very long. When I call my sister, I assuage my conscience by telling myself that if we lived near each other, we'd go out to lunch, and that would cost more than a phone call. But phone calls are ephemeral. Once you've hung up, it's over. A letter, however, can be held in the hand. You can enjoy it again the next day.

Writing has another advantage over telephoning because you can make a rough draft and rewrite. It allows you to take your foot out of your mouth before mailing the letter—unless you're like me and mail the original letter, foot and all. You can even keep the letter for a day or two, and see if you still want to mail it. Mistakes in tact—maybe even lawsuits—can be avoided by waiting twenty-four hours.

Etiquette maven Letitia Baldridge offers specific advice for letter writers, such as writing in a pleasant and comfortable place and always writing at a specially appointed time. And that you shouldn't be interrupted. (How is that managed?) She also recommends using a good pen and some favorite stationery.

Good grief. I'd never write a letter if I had to satisfy all those conditions. That's like scheduling sex for 2:15 on Thursdays.

My letters tend to happen early in the morning while I still have on my wet swimsuit from my 7:30 A.M. trek to the swimming pool. I go to my desk to see what's on my list for the day, and then, somehow, I'll be sitting on the already water-stained desk chair, tinking away at the typewriter, three pages already, too many, correcting with my Pilot Razor Point pen, and there, it's done. I can't help letter writing.

When you sit down to write, don't write about the weather or say that you must hurry and get this in the mail before the mailman comes. Write about yourself—what you've been doing, thinking, observing, hoping, and planning. Add some gossip. In addition to responses to his or her last letter, the reader wants news. The personal letter can be news for the writer, too—a focus of self-knowledge.

If letter writing is too intimidating, write postcards, plain or with pictures. Local postcards with a short message—a club reminder, maybe—are a good alternative for phone calls, too. They don't take as long, and the recipient has something in hand.

I collect postcards when I'm traveling. They are a good hobby because they're easy to pack. I've learned to buy two of each—one to keep and one to mail. Who knows? Someday they might be valuable, like old comic books. In any case, write on!

How to Know Whether You Are an Oldie

To my delight, I ran across a publication especially for those of us who are old enough to balance our checkbooks without a calculator.

The magazine is called *The Oldie*, comes from London, and properly attacks young people—or at least youthfulness. The cover sports a triangular road sign that was once used by the British Department of Transport until they were forced to drop it because it was thought to be offensive to older people. Now graduated to the magazine, the red triangle encloses a drawing of two doddering oldies, one with a cane. At last we have magazine that isn't unrelentingly cheerful. Old fogies, after all, are allowed to grouse a little.

In one article titled, "Rage," Auberon Waugh writes, "Sex is, of course, an important subject, but it is so well covered elsewhere that I do not see that *The Oldie* need mention it much." Then he goes on to discuss it at length. He feels that people turn to *The Oldie* to escape from sex. He also wonders—in a cynical voice—what the penalty is for exposing oneself, and how many times a week he could afford it on his pension.

Angela Huth writes in *The Oldie* that she has a tough time getting someone to do a hairstyle that doesn't look like a Brillo pad such as the young people wear. She goes back to her old hairdresser, Patricia, who sympathizes with her. "Modern salons are very insecure, arrogant and unwelcoming," Patricia says. "They are full of little Napoleons with absolutely no sense of humor. Most of them aren't remotely interested in anyone over twenty-five."

So how do you know when you've become an oldie? For one thing, when you get an invitation to join AARP, you know you're living on the edge. Of course, they seem to be sending out notices to younger and younger people, all of whom are enraged.

Take this test to learn whether you are an oldie. You know you are an oldie if you:

- Think mousse is something you make out of chocolate and egg whites, not a hair dressing.
- Own an orangewood stick.
- Saw *Casablanca* when it first came out.
- Say the time is "quarter to four" rather than "three forty-five."
- Know how to make gravy and never call it "sauce."
- Use the backs of envelopes for your grocery list rather than buying little multicolored notepads.
- Think long-distance phone calls are for important matters.
- Think your spouse looks great with white hair.
- Are amazed to learn that the golden oldies radio station plays modern music from the sixties instead of oldies music from the forties.
- Think of Jack Parr as the host of *The Tonight Show* rather than what's-his-name.
- Know a noun from a verb.
- Repair hems with needle and thread rather than tape.
- Know the words to "Always."
- Learned to drive on a stick-shift car.
- Remember when Frank Sinatra had hair.
- Remember Frank Sinatra.
- Think brassieres should be worn *under* your clothes not on top, Madonna style.

- Have pictures in your photo album of people you don't recognize.
- Know what RSVP means.
- Avoid Early Bird Specials because everyone knows what the early bird gets.
- Know in your heart you are not old enough to read *Modern Maturity* magazine.

Your Score . . .

If you agree with five or fewer statements: You are a Neo-Oldie.

If you agree with five to ten statements: You are an Oldie in Good Standing.

If you agree with more than ten statements: You are a Distinguished Oldie.

The New Smoking Etiquette

Smoking has always been a favorite pastime for oldies, along with drinking and carousing. Just look at the old black-and-white movies. Smoking was classy. Think of *The Thin Man*. Everybody smoked except Asta. Try to imagine Humphrey Bogart without a cigarette. Of course, Humphrey Bogart is now what *The Oldie* magazine calls a former oldie (dead), but there you go. You can't win 'em all.

Smokers don't even ask for ashtrays anymore. The baby boomers have gotten rid of them. Smokers, who used to be the leaders of society, have now become a mere subset. You see them standing in huddled masses outside building entrances, young and old, furtively sharing their common avocation. Exiled to doorways and benches, they are no longer acceptable to polite society.

It's hard to not feel sorry for them, they look so downtrodden. But if a friendly smile is offered—I'm okay, you're okay—they duck their heads toward the hand from which hangs the burning ember of their addiction.

Banned from smoking indoors, they are now allowed to escape, which is what smoking is all about: a moment to interrupt the routine, a self-indulgence, a brief interlude for meditation. Meanwhile, their coworkers, clean and unaddicted, are still indoors, pushing pencils or merchandise in closed spaces while the smokers are outdoors relaxing in the sunshine and fresh air.

The little groups standing in doorways have developed their own networking system. Smokers have no discriminatory practices. Old and young, male and female, blacks and whites, Christians and Jews are all welcomed under the communal awning in fair weather and foul. Strange alliances are born. The vice president and the maintenance worker compare notes on child-care centers. The personnel director and the mail clerk share anecdotes about their dogs. Gossip is exchanged between the hierarchy and the underlings. The smokers network has been known to initiate promotions, love affairs.

New York cynic Fran Lebowitz writes in her book, *Social Studies*: "Smoking is, if not my life, then at least my hobby. I love to smoke. Smoking is fun. Smoking is cool. Smoking is, as far as I'm concerned, the entire point of being an adult. It makes growing up genuinely worthwhile."

You have to respect someone who flies in the face of both logic and public opinion.

Some smokers are fighting back. An oldie smoker reportedly refused to refrain from smoking at her condominium clubhouse meeting. She said she would smoke wherever and as often as she wanted to. She pridefully said she came from a family of smokers and drinkers. Her resistance created a fiery explosion, with talk of lawyers being summoned and people sulking with their arms crossed over their chests. Local newspapers reported the uproar.

There are distinct advantages to the new smoking etiquette. Escape, for instance. At meetings or parties, certain participants will disappear for a few minutes. The hostess will be in the kitchen, trying to keep the hollandaise from separating, and will notice that she is alone. In the living room, the group has quietly thinned.

The remaining nonsmokers bravely carry on with the conversation, wishing *they* were somewhere else, wondering if dinner will *ever* be served, trying to think how *they* can escape this party. Meanwhile, smokers have been given permission to simply get up and walk out without a word.

In restaurants, the smoking area is always preferable to the non-smoking area. The lighting is better—not so harsh—the decorations are more graceful, and the mood is one of camaraderie and conviviality. All the interesting people are sitting in the smoking section.

It takes audacity and tenacity to be a smoker these days. But someday, smokers will hold their heads high again, laughing as they linger over their luxury, suddenly realizing that they have become the elite once again. It would not be excessive to assume they might sponsor a float in the annual Doo-Dah Parade next January.

One nonsmoking oldie brags that he has profited for years from stock in one of the tobacco companies and is pleased when he sees people smoking. "Smoking," he says at every opportunity, "is a good hobby for people in wheelchairs."

And a chest surgeon posts a sign in his waiting room that reads, "Please smoke. It's good for business."

Garage Sales

The garage sale must be an American invention. It's difficult to visualize a European woman putting stained sweaters and dented electric can openers on a table in the driveway, assuming her neighbors will find them desirable.

We Americans have a lot of confidence in our own taste, and not only that, we are a very generous people—willing to sell a limp and faded blouse for only seventy-five cents, and a hardback copy of *Passages* for fifty cents.

Have you ever been to a garage sale that did *not* have a copy of *Passages?* It must be the symbol of garage sales all over the country. A book concerning the changes that take place in life, it is read by people who then apparently decide to have a major crisis of their own. They decide to sell the house, get a divorce, remodel, or sponsor some other kind of personal upheaval, giving them the opportunity to have a garage sale.

These household purges are typical of our generation. I don't remember people having garage sales when I was a child in the 1930s and 1940s. The Great Depression was either still on us or not far in the past, so there was no impulse to discard belongings. We were still using them. That was in the days when recycling was so routine it didn't even have a name. My mother saved everything. She didn't buy books, but she did save *Reader's Digest.* Socks were darned, hems let down, faded clothing dyed with Rit. She saved the tiniest bits of food and made leftovers out of leftovers—and still had leftovers—which used to puzzle her a great deal. It was the fishes-and-loaves syndrome. Nothing was let go.

Not long ago, I had to move my now eighty-eight-year-old mother from her own apartment into a retirement residence where she would receive some nursing care. A lot of her belongings went with her, but some had to be recycled. My sister and I had to decide what to keep, what to discard, what to share with grandchildren.

I fell heir to a heavy old, brown stoneware mixing bowl. It's not attractive, but I remember it was always in my mother's kitchen. She put bread dough in it to rise. And the bowl's thick edge made a good surface for sharpening knives. The old brown bowl had first been my grandmother's, and therefore had seen duty in a sod house on the North Dakota prairie. It might have come from Russia. I'm glad it didn't disappear in a garage sale.

Not long ago, we renovated (read: gutted and started over) a small cottage on my son's property in northern California. We call it The Mom and Pop Motel or sometimes Relative Comfort. It was relatively comfortable considering it had no heat. I shopped for a few pieces of furniture, not at garage sales, but at secondhand stores and found a dear little desk and chair and also an old chest for a coffee table. The chest has iron fittings and looks as if it has a history. It's obviously traveled a lot, maybe on ships.

Old things can either get shabby or more valuable. Do we get better or worse as we get older? It depends on the original quality. Just because we're getting old doesn't mean we are hallowed or deserve respect. Some oldies are wise, some are silly old fools, but most are probably no better or worse than we ever were. If set out at a garage sale, none of us would bring much more than seventy-five cents.

Oldie on Campus

Intergenerational conflict isn't something I think about. Young people have been kind to me as I have become long of tooth.

In 1975, when I was forty-five, I went back to college to complete my B.A. I thought I might feel out of place in a classroom with twenty-year-olds. But no one ever alluded to the fact that I was old enough to be their mother. If I had something to talk about, they were perfectly willing to sit and talk to me like anyone else in the class. Those were exciting times with lots of new ideas.

In those days, we wore jeans, faded shirts, and platform high-heeled shoes. Being soigné was not in. Neither were spandex pants. We sat around in the student lounge and put our feet on the already distressed coffee tables. Beer was sold at the snack bar, and pool games were in progress at one end of the long room. There was a smell of coffee and Chee·tos and mildewed rugs. And sometimes of sweaty socks.

It seems to me now that I grew up in room 101B, around the corner and down the hall from the student lounge. I don't recall feeling older than the other students. In fact, I felt young and unformed, like a larvae learning to weave its cocoon. I felt tender and exposed, still learning to function in the twentieth century even though I had sons about the same age as my classmates.

I don't mean to imply that there were no differences. I remember a young man looking at me in alarm when I told him that sex was between his ears, not between his legs. We must have been discussing either *Madame Bovary* or his social life. He was the same young man who had a beat-up Volkswagen bug with a bashed place in the rear. He glued an old tennis shoe into the depression. I thought it terribly creative and witty. He was a poet, but I think he went astray and transferred to the business school because it was more practical. Another American tragedy.

And where are the people who were with me on the little magazine we put out once or twice? I remember a vibrant young woman who had a small child. Her writing showed the poignancy of working, going to school, and raising a child alone. And there was a perpetual student whose hair turned grey before he stopped changing majors and finally graduated. At least I think he graduated. Maybe he's still there.

And there was an elderly couple—is it all right to say elderly? Did we decide what to call old people? If it's all right to say young, why isn't it all right to say old?—who remembered when the Buster Keaton movies first came out. Those two people were a wonderful addition to our classes.

Many of my friends today are people I met there. They were also nontraditional students.

Although I resisted graduating, I finally had to take the required freshman math and be on my way. When I took algebra in high school, we didn't even *have* negative numbers. I didn't know what was happening in college algebra. I cried for a while and then decided to drop out and take dumbbell algebra instead. I remember the math coach telling the class that algebra was important because it would help us solve problems in life. After class, I told the eighteen-year-old students that I had never used any math that I learned after the fifth grade and had not found algebra valuable in Marriage and the Family 101. My background as a nurse, however, had been invaluable training for life.

I wrote a sonnet for the math coach—who was twenty years younger than I—about the futility of taking algebra. He loved it, but I don't think he understood it. I got a C and was glad to have it. After algebra, I took one semester of logic, which was wonderful. That's where I learned how to win arguments.

I don't have intergenerational conflicts with people older than me, either. I admit, I get annoyed at people who drive their cars twenty-five miles per hour in a forty-mile-per-hour zone, and at people who make left turns from the right lane. But they aren't all old. Sometimes they're just tourists.

One of the things I like about old people is the way they say what they think. I guess they figure that if they're too old to risk buying green bananas, they're too old to care whether other people agree with them or not. Maybe I'll be better at being old than at being fifty or sixty.

Eccentricity

The best part of being an oldie is that you get to be eccentric and young people have to be polite and patronize your idiosyncrasies. Young people are loosely defined as those who remember watching *Romper Room* in their jammies. This group includes my editor. (Romper stomper bomper boo. I can see our friends at home. Can you?) Oh, all right. As a mom, I watched it. But not in my jammies.

Today, the august and revered Little Old Lady who is in tennis shoes might be wearing Nikes, but we are also seeing a lot of Keds again—plain white and classic. I have a new pair myself.

I tried on and refused to buy those athletic shoes that make you look as if you've broken your lower leg and are wearing orthopedic splints. "I hate these," I said to the salesman who had a spike hairstyle. "I can't walk in them." I felt rooted to the ground. The tongues came to midcalf. The salesman was appalled that I balked at buying the shoes, especially since they were such a good price, only $69.95. I looked longingly at the white Keds, but the salesman, who was backed up by a woman at the rear of the store who seemed to be his mother—said they could not, in good conscience, sell me the Keds because they would not give me adequate support. You don't have to be old to be eccentric.

David Weeks, an American psychologist working in Scotland, is researching eccentrics. He reports that eccentrics are curious and creative, often with high IQs, and are usually quite happy. Women were noted as becoming eccentric later in life than men, usually after the children have left home.

The following are some suggestions on how to be eccentric.

♦ Make your own mayonnaise and offer to give your children the recipe. Tell them it's easy. If they roll their eyes and say, "Oh, Mom," just cackle.

♦ At the grocery store, tell complete strangers why the produce is so much better and cheaper in New York. Say that no one is serious about their work in Florida. If the stranger looks nervous, talk louder and follow him or her around to the bananas.

♦ Refuse to buy Christmas presents, but buy a lot of birthday presents. Send five birthday cards instead of one.

♦ Win a samba contest.

♦ Collect cats. The animal shelter recently advertised, Cats: Half Price. This is a good opportunity to buy enough to make a good grouping around the cat-food dish.

♦ Treat your maladies with old remedies. If you have an upset stomach, take eight drops of belladonna in an ounce of water. Take oatmeal baths or sunbaths for skin rashes instead of cortisone cream. Grow your own aloe, and rub a broken piece on a burn.

♦ Insist that door-to-door evangelists give you a five-dollar donation for *your* church before you'll listen to their spiel. (I've tried it. It works.) Or ask them for their address so *you* can harass *them* another day.

♦ Take photographs of everyone who comes to your house. This includes the evangelists, the bug spray man, the woman who brings the new phone book, the electrician, your mother-in-law, and the cookie agents.

♦ Take your lunch in a paper bag on airplanes. I used to think that was eccentric, but it's becoming common. See. I was right.

- Better yet, travel by train or bus. You'll see more and will meet a lot of eccentrics.
- Be in love with the oldie with glow-in-the-dark white hair who sleeps next to you.
- Be good to yourself. That's the whole point of being eccentric. But you knew all this stuff already.

A House by the Side of the Road

Let me live in my house by the side of the road, and be a friend to man.
—Sam Walter Foss

It might be a southern custom, this sitting in the garage, watching the world go by. I've noticed that people, sometimes one, sometimes a pair, put up their garage door, bring out aluminum folding chairs, and sit partly in and partly out of the garage in the shade of the door. They might have a comfortable porch, but they prefer garage sitting. Once in a while, I'll see one of them holding the hose and watering the nearby bushes or grass as they sit.

A few months ago a variation in the garage-sitting theme began to appear. I can't remember if the gazebo came first or the white picket fence, but it was the ornate fence that caught my eye.

It was stretched across the front of an open garage and had a hinged gate. The garage itself was partitioned off, as if remodeled. All that remained was an area five or six feet deep. In front of this garage remainder was the white fence. The next time I went by, I saw an easy chair behind the fence—not just a folding chair, but an upholstered chair. Later, a television set appeared on the wall opposite the chair.

It must have been about that time that the lacy gazebo, a romantic Victorian-style summerhouse, appeared in the front yard. I couldn't stand it any longer. My curiosity got the best of me.

Enter Henry F. La Flamme, woodworker and garage-sitter extraordinaire. When I pulled into his driveway, he was sitting in the garage without the TV on. It was a cloudy day, a little rainy, and quiet on the street.

La Flamme is a seventy-five-year-old widower, wiry and spry with a smile like a sunrise, bright and warm and welcoming. I learned that he made the fence and gazebo on his workbench in the backyard. When he told me he was a professional carpenter, I was not surprised.

La Flamme opened the little gate and brushed off a grey swivel office chair for me to sit on. His portly dachshund, Queenie, wiggled nimbly up beside him in the easy chair and looked at me with intelligent eyes, as if she were taking part in the conversation.

In addition to the two comfortable chairs and the television mounted on the wall, there was a small radio on a shelf built for it, an expandable reading lamp, a yellow wall telephone behind La Flamme's head, and a sign that read, Ask Me to Tell You about My Grandchildren. On the floor beside me was a miniature bed for Queenie with carved posts and a red-and-blue plaid blanket. Queenie stirred nervously when I examined her bed.

Fastened to the wall, near La Flamme's right hand, was a curved brass holder. He said he got it at a garage sale, and he thinks it's a flowerpot holder, but he has put a green metal ashtray in it and uses it for the Pall Malls he smokes. "I probably smoke too much," he said, "but what else have I got to do while I watch the ten o'clock news, the eleven o'clock news?"

He looks hearty, but says he is "battery operated" and has an "eye implant." He mows both his own lawn and his neighbors', and rides a three-wheel bike to the shopping center.

Why does he prefer sitting in the garage to his comfortable home?

"We don't want to be stuck in back of the house all day," he says, petting Queenie. "A lot of people stop on the road to look at the gazebo. I've met some real nice people." His warm smile shows how much he enjoys visitors.

The white gazebo in the front yard is intricately carved and decorated and even has a chandelier that is lit at night. Why doesn't he sit in the gazebo? "I don't want to *sit* in it," he says. "I want to *look* at it."

La Flamme clearly enjoys his work as much as his leisure. "When you enjoy it, it isn't work," he says.

La Flamme has taken a common leisure custom and turned it into an art form. He remains active in the parade of life by maintaining his skills and identity. He's having fun, too. "I might slow down when I'm ninety," he says.

Sleep Patterns

Sleeping has always been my favorite hobby, but lately, my sleep patterns have changed. Maybe this is because of my age. I think of the classic image of Grandma, dozing over her knitting in the rocking chair. I'll admit to being a granny and to knitting, but my naps are usually taken sprawling on the couch with a newspaper falling from my hand and a cat on my belly.

If left undisturbed by the radio alarm in the morning, I'd sleep ten hours. This has nothing to do with age. I've always needed a lot of sleep. Now, however, I luxuriate in a charade of being too sophisticated to watch television. "I'm going upstairs to read," I announce haughtily, stomping up the steps at nine o'clock. I tote books, a newspaper, and a magazine up the steps, make myself comfortable, and then punch up a couple of pillows. I plan the course of reading: short-duty things first, then a longer piece. This is all theatrics. I'm asleep with the light in my eyes in ten minutes.

Between 1:00 and 3:00 A.M., the room now dark, my eyes pop open, and I'm all chat, either actually or in my head, rehearsing the past day or planning the next, remembering what I forgot to do and what I did wrong. My brain might natter at me with trivial or real concerns for as long as two hours. Then I'll fall soundly asleep again until the radio wakes me at 5:30. As soon as I hear the music, I stick my head under the pillow, now uninterested in all the things that were important at 3:00 A.M.

I've been thinking that if this pattern continues, I should make use of it. I might as well give in to the idea that I'm tired by 9:00 and need to sleep then. Why, however, should the hours in the middle of the night be wasted? I could get up and do any number of things. I could do the reading that is by now chronically unfinished, or I could write letters. I could balance my checkbook, take out the trash, or clean out the hall closet or the kitchen cupboards. I could finish the sweater I started knitting in November. Last night I thought I'd love to get up and go for a walk, the air was so soft and sweet and the moon so bright.

The man I sleep with (we've been married for forty years) is often awake at night, too. He, however, is able to empty his mind with meditation or willpower or pure perverseness and goes back to sleep. Or we might stay awake and talk. Night talk used to be whispered, but now with no children in the house to disturb, we just talk out loud. It seems illegal somehow, but it is one of the privileges of age.

This morning during tooth brushing, I said, "We spend too much time in bed, going to bed so early."

"Yes," he said. "Isn't it wonderful?"

Over the Hill at Sixty-Two

A thirty-five-year-old friend asked me if I was still enjoying the smaller house that we moved into a few years ago. "Aren't you concerned about going up and down stairs as you get older?" she asked. I'm sixty-two.

"No," I said. "I ride my bike to the pool three days a week and then swim a mile. On alternate days, I walk two miles and then do a half hour of yoga, so I'm still able to climb the stairs."

The same week, a fifty-three-year-old friend said to me, "At sixty-two, you only have about fifteen good years left."

Both of these people are good and true friends, so although I was surprised by their remarks at first, I realized that they were not being unkind. What they were saying did have a grain—or more—of truth: I'm not getting any younger.

I've decided not to age gracefully. I think I'll be snappish and develop a quavery voice. Carrying a cane might be a nice touch. I enjoyed the senior who once rapped on the hood of my car with his cane when I stopped too close to the crosswalk at a red light. And now I can say anything I want to because, with so little time left, I'm too old to care if people get mad at me. What have I got to lose?

A seventy-year-old widow said she was fed up with the holidays and was going away for Christmas next year. She told her children she was taking off.

"If that's what you want to do, that's all right, Mother," her son said.

"You're darn right it is," she said. "And if it isn't, there isn't much you can do about it."

I think I'll start calling people things like "young lady" and "sonny."

For instance, I could call my doctor young lady instead of Susan. Or my attorney could be sonny instead of Jim. Has a nice ring to it, doesn't it?

Speaking of attorneys, maybe I should start writing people in and out of my will, especially right after the holidays. I understand that's when a lot of people who feel they've been slighted for one reason or another decide to take definitive action.

Or I could start giving away trinkets that I never use to remind people of how frail I am and to try to garner sympathy and attention. "Here, you can have my cut-glass marmalade jar. At my age, I won't need it much longer."

But I haven't got time to start these projects this week. I've got too many other things to do. There's the swimming and what not, and I have some writing projects on the back burner, and I'm trying to fulfill my new year's resolution of going to more movies (cheaper for me now, to my delight). I'll get old and crotchety another time. I can hardly wait.

Becoming Curmudgeonly

An Ann Landers column carried a Gem of the Day reading: "This card was phoned to a florist: 'Thank you for just being you. The year you were Cleopatra, you were a mess.'"

That's us. That's the oldies over fifty. We don't have to be Cleopatra anymore. It's too late to impress people. We can just be ourselves now. So who are we? Carl Jung was accused of saying, "Everybody's who he or she was in third grade."

I was a weenie in third grade. Every day I prayed for a fire drill during arithmetic. I lived only for library period. Sure enough, I haven't changed a bit. I'm a Friend of the Library, and I still count on my fingers.

It takes time to know who we are and to be comfortable with that. It's a happy revelation when we get that *aha!* feeling. Suddenly, we know that we are never going to break one hundred—or even 120—on the golf course and don't want to try. We go back to doing what we feel good doing: playing the flute maybe, or walking slowly to the park early in the morning with a mug of coffee.

For me, it was learning that I didn't have to play bridge. When I was twenty-five, everyone played. I learned, sort of. Then my mother-in-law invited me to a bridge luncheon for thirty women. I spent the afternoon playing cards, failing, as usual, to see the importance of games.

Later, my mother-in-law said, "Either take some lessons and learn to play well, or don't play."

I was electrified. I had a choice?

If you threaten a competitive person with "Play or else," he or she will be hell-bent to sign up for lessons. It didn't work with me. I quit playing. My mother-in-law was exasperated, but I was finding out that being Cleopatra was not for me. That was the beginning. From then on, I knew that I could make choices and be who I was, not someone others wanted me to be.

As we get older, we aren't so worried about what people will think of us. When a friend had uninvited houseguests who didn't leave after several days, he decided he would have to say something to them about it. They wanted to party at night, and he had to get up and go to work every morning. In the car, driving home from work, he rehearsed what he would say to them. But when he got there, he simply said, "Hey, you guys are going to have to leave. You're driving me crazy. I'm not on vacation. You are. I've got to work and I'm worn out."

His guests said, "Oh. Okay."

We've had our friends for so long now that we can speak frankly without destroying the friendship. We don't have to agree with each other about everything, but we can remain friends. In fact, we relish the contrasts.

You can see where this is leading. We're now well seasoned enough that we are becoming curmudgeons—or termagants, a comparable female form. According to Jon Winokur, a curmudgeon is "(1) a crusty, ill-tempered, churlish old man; (2) anyone who hates hypocrisy and pretense and has the temerity to say so."

Jon Winokur writes in his book, *The Portable Curmudgeon,* "Curmudgeons are like sumo wrestlers. It takes a long time and a lot of abuse to make one."

Yeah, and proud of it, too.

Older Than Sixty-Five

At the shopping center, a man sat on a bench under the arcade. He looked as if he might be in his eighties—bent, thin-limbed, sparse white hair. A woman of about the same age approached and greeted him.

"It was nice your mother came to visit you," I overheard her say to him.

"Yes," he responded, "I'm going down to Miami to see *her* next month."

His *mother,* I thought. How old is *she?*

The term *older generation* takes on new meanings in the 1990s. There are the old, the older, and the oldest. Lumping everyone older than sixty-five into one group is like saying everyone under sixty-five is about the same age. A twenty-year-old would be surprised to be included in the under sixty-five group—or even to be compared to a forty-year-old.

The older generation is several generations, too, not just one. There is a generation of experiences between sixty-year-olds and ninety-year-olds, not just physical differences and abilities.

This line at sixty-five was imposed by our bureaucracy which designates sixty-five as old, or at least old enough for Social Security. That's when we're expected to retire. At sixty-five, the government considers all of us legally over the hill.

At the turn of the century, sixty-five *was* old. Although some lived long lives, many of our grandparents died in their forties. Today, it is not unusual for seventy-year-olds to be caring for their parents. I once talked to a man in a retirement care facility who daily walked two blocks to another facility to visit his mother. He complained that she was still telling him what to wear.

When my mother was seventy-five, she considered *me* a spring chicken at fifty. Actually, I did too. I was just hitting my stride.

People in their fifth and sixth decades are among the movers and shakers of our society. Some are at their peak and just reaching their goals in life. They are business moguls, politicians, teachers, and chairmen and chairwomen of the board. Among them are shop owners and managers. Their eighty-year-old parents might still be on the golf course, in the classroom again, or doing consulting work. Or doing the same work they've done all their lives.

Some things transcend age. Advertisers are beginning to realize that older age does not mean fewer sales. A Banana Republic ad shows two handsome and distinguished elders in casual clothing. Everyone, two or ninety-two, can wear jeans and camp shirts. The manufacturers are finally noticing that we are out here, and we buy clothes. There are more and more of us, and we have more money than the two-year-olds.

Collecting all of us on one side or the other of sixty-five only works for Social Security.

I'm Not Going

One of the delights known to age, and beyond the grasp of youth, is that of "not going."
—J. B. Priestly

Jean Herman said she wasn't going, and she meant it. I admire the woman who refused to move out of her small apartment in New York City to make way for a high-rise office building.

She apparently refused $750,000 to vacate her $200-a-month apartment. The building had been her home for thirty years. And by New York law, tenants of rent-controlled apartments cannot be evicted except under certain circumstances.

Herman's portion of the building was left standing even though the rest of it was torn down. Her solitary brownstone now stands out from the towering new office building. The construction noise must have been terrible and the utilities occasionally had to be cut off. But she stayed until she died in 1992 at the age of sixty-nine—an American heroine.

This modern-day *Bartleby the Scrivener* made her choice, dug in her heels, and endured. Other tenants sold out for big bucks, but she, like Herman Melville's Bartleby, preferred not to.

Her brother said he didn't know why she wouldn't move. Her lawyer said she was opposed to overdevelopment on principle, and she was also eccentric.

Let's hear it for eccentric. And for making choices.

That's what liberty is all about—the freedom to make choices. Liberty is a lofty and decorous word, one that we do not often use outside political, sports, or religious arenas. We make speeches and sing songs about liberty, but not many have the courage to implement it. For one thing, you have to take responsibility yourself, and most people would like to have someone else be responsible—the insurance company or the government or the landlord.

Liberty isn't easy. Making choices and living with the consequences is demanding. I have no doubt that Ms. Herman must have had days when she wondered why she had given herself the liberty of making this choice and whether she had made a mistake. Did she ever think about what she might have done with the $750,000?

Apparently, she found that her familiar apartment suited her well. It was her home. She preferred not to move. Once you get it right, why compromise?

Being American

As is the custom at a party, I joined a small group of people already in conversation. They were talking about the modern American Indian. A beautiful young woman explained to me, "I'm a Cherokee, but I'm an urban Indian."

Like many, I'm enchanted with the romantic idea of Indians, or Native Americans, even though I haven't made a study of their cultures. Meeting a full-blooded Cherokee really knocked my socks off. (I was disappointed that she wore no feathers and had no flint-tipped weapons in sight, but I didn't say anything to her about that.)

It occurred to me once again that no matter how long we have lived in America, we still claim other roots. Even the one nonimmigrant American in this group claimed another national division—Cherokee—and broke down her identity even more finely—urban.

"What nationality are you?" is a frequent conversational topic. When asked this recently by a robust young woman, I answered, "I'm an American."

"I know," she said, "but where are you from?"

I said I was from Colorado, but seeing her blank stare, I said that I had been born in America and so had my parents. None of us had ever been to Denmark or Germany where *their* parents had come from.

"I knew you were Scandinavian!" she crowed.

"I've never been to Denmark, I don't speak the language, can't stand cold weather, and have never tasted lutefisk." I'm not sure I can spell it, either.

"But it's in your blood," she said.

She wouldn't give up, so I did.

This "What is your nationality?" game is beginning to get silly. Having grown up in the Southwest, I feel more in tune with Spanish cultures than I do with northern European cultures. On the other hand, I have also learned to enjoy pita bread, sukiyaki, cheese blintzes, huaraches, and Haitian cotton. But creamed peas and bucolic landscapes leave me cold.

My mother, however, is closer to her immigrant parents, still laces her food with cream and butter, and never has chili pepper in her kitchen. I tried to teach her to make barbecued ribs once. She wanted to learn because her grandsons like barbecue. She never quite got the hang of it. She tended to stew the ribs in ketchup rather than dry roasting and basting with spicy sauce.

If you carry this nationality phenomenon one step further, consider what my grandchildren would have to say if they answered the nationality question as required. They are the products of four generations of American marriages and would have to answer, "Danish, German, Swedish, Norwegian, English, French, American Indian, Greenlander, Italian, and Polish."

We could say that we are native American because we were born here, but that would be misleading. I have no objections to being just plain American. In fact, I love it. The rubbing against different cultures gives us a certain patina, and I think it wears well. Having lived in the Philippine Islands for three years, I learned that I did, indeed, have a national identity of my own. In foreign countries, Americans are accepted as real flesh and blood people without ornamenting themselves with the totems of their ancestors. Try telling the customs officer that you are Danish or German while carrying an American passport.

Some Americans have been here shorter lengths of time, or their families are more closely aligned with their parental origins. A first-generation American whose parents are Italian, for instance, feels the strength of the Italian culture more than a third- or fourth-generation American whose forbears came from England. Some nationalities make more of an effort to maintain their former cultures and have tighter family liaisons than others. But as Americans, we tend to mix and blend, to share our recipes, our slang, and our love.

Although clinging to my American identity, I know that it is impossible to totally decant the mixture that we are. That mixture includes cultures we have assimilated that have nothing to do with family. For example, my affinity to Spanish cultures. Even my new Indian friend defines herself as an *urban* Cherokee, a learned culture that her grandparents were probably not part of.

Somehow, "What tribe are you?" sounds better and makes more sense than "What nationality are you?" I guess it means the same thing, but tribe seems to imply a part of a whole. It sounds more, well, American.

None of us can or will give up our uniqueness, and that's an all-American trait. There are even some Americans who claim Texas as their country of origin.

One-Hour Photos

Oldies like to think of themselves as curmudgeons. Only a misguided few are incessantly cheerful, and those people must be avoided at all costs. Don't criticize them, just realize they can't help it.

Being disillusioned with the modern world is our favorite hobby—no, it's our responsibility—and we are never satisfied with circumstances. One of our complaints is the contradictions in our lives. For instance, it's wonderful to have modern conveniences like one-hour film developing at the shopping center. Just a few years ago (in oldie lingo, *few* is translated as *forty*), it took a week to see how many heads we'd cut off in the family Christmas photos, but today our lack of focus on life's happenings is reproduced on the same day as the transgression.

Or at least that's what the sign says. But do you know of anyone for whom this has actually transpired? Have you *ever* had film developed in one hour?

Early one Sunday afternoon, I took some film to be developed. I was very anxious to have the pictures because I had given my four-year-old granddaughter one of those disposable cameras and told her to take pictures at a birthday party she attended. I wanted to see the world from the viewpoint of a four-year-old. She is, of course, a clever and advanced four-year-old, and I knew it would be a new art form. I wanted the photos so I could brag to friends at dinner that evening.

"They'll be ready Tuesday," said the teenage clerk at the drugstore where I bought the film.

"I want them this afternoon," I said. "Your sign says one-hour service."

"You want them today?" He sounded surprised but did some calcu-
lations in his head.

"That's gonna cost ya $10.19. But it'll be a while. Five o'clock,
pro'lly."

"How much if I get them Tuesday?"

"Uh. That'll cost ya $10.19."

I'm suffering from confusion at this point and give in to what seems
an excessive price because I want the almost-instant gratification that
has been advertised. "Well. All right. I need them today. Two prints in
the small size, please."

"Two prints? That'll cost ya $14.90. Anyway, we don't make the
small size, only the big ones."

"Forget it. I'm taking them to the grocery store." As I stormed
toward the door, he yelled, "It'll cost ya more there."

At the supermarket there was a special: two prints, small size, $3.09,
but not until Tuesday. I went for it.

The circumstances here turned out to my advantage. In the end, I
got a good buy, and everybody knows that one-hour photo doesn't exist
anyway. It's a fantasy, a merchandising mirage. I had won the price war.
According to the rules, however, I had every right to be grumpy and to
complain about my original frustration to everyone I met, especially to
my friends at dinner. The developing price was high, the service not as
advertised, the clerk surly. There was the inconvenience of going to
another store. And there was something for everyone in the anecdote.
My friends were pleased because they got to hear a lot of complaining
about modern days and young people—without the added annoyance of
having to look at pictures taken by a four-year old.

Seize the Day

One of my favorite English professors used to say, and probably still does, "We're all terminal cases. We just don't know what day we'll die."

On our down days, we are afraid of death, or if not death, we are afraid of *how* we will die, which is the scary part. Dying is more difficult for some than others. Some have physical problems for a long time, treatable to varying degrees, while others die suddenly, when taking the milk from the refrigerator. We all want to die quickly, as if struck by lightning. Not everyone is that lucky.

A Gallup poll reports that for the first time in history, half of the deaths in America are due to self-inflicted injuries—smoking, drinking, and poor health habits.

It's very hard to think about your own death. Your mind digs in its heels and skids to a stop. Shortly before his death, John Steinbeck said he knew everyone had to die, but he'd always thought an exception would be made in his case.

My philosophy about life and death is *carpe diem:* seize the day. This is not just a clever T-shirt graffito. It came from the Roman poet, Horace, born in 65 B.C. The whole phrase is: "Seize the day, put no trust in the morrow." Someone else said it this way: "Life is short. Eat your dessert first." How I love a cynic.

My father, who is now in a nursing home with Alzheimer's disease, seized his days as well as he could. He liked bacon and eggs followed by an oatmeal cookie for breakfast, but he didn't smoke or drink much, played golf a lot, took a nap after lunch, and went to church regularly.

Later in life, he did some wandering, traveling around the country in a small travel trailer.

He hasn't known any of us for almost five years. It was heartbreaking when I saw him a month or so ago and tried to tell him that he has a great-granddaughter, but I could not penetrate the Alzheimer's barrier. I do not apologize for saying that I hope for his death soon. This is not the way my father would choose to live. It is not, in fact, living.

Because we don't have a whole lot of choice about how we die— some, but not a lot—we should concentrate on living well while we can. We should make as many choices as we can about how we conduct our lives. We should choose to be as healthy as possible by eating well and getting exercise. If we feel well, we will enjoy ourselves more. But remember, there is more to life than cholesterol.

Be a sensualist: See, hear, smell, touch, and taste. I'm not talking about daily bacchanals, but if you can work that into your schedule from time to time, maybe you should. If you've always wanted to go to New Zealand, do it if you possibly can. If not, read everything you can find about it.

Call an old friend to hear how life turned out. Go to the movies in the afternoon—alone—and relish the fact that you are playing hooky and no one knows where you are. Wear soft clothes. Sleep nude.

Learn to tap dance, call room service, refuse to go to receptions for dignitaries. Have leftover pumpkin pie with whipped cream for breakfast as often as possible—well, at least once a year. Savor the scent of jasmine in May and pine in December. Do *not* come in out of the rain.

Remember that living well is the best revenge.

Seven Deadly Sins

Florida is hotter than hell in July, which makes me think of the seven deadly sins. Oldies have tried the seven deadly sins and enjoyed them all. We could give lessons.

Pride is paramount. Never hesitate to instruct the young about the value of hard work and frugality. Take pride in being able to help them with your own good examples and accomplishments. Be sure to tell them about how it was in the depression. They've heard it before, but they never tire of it.

Justifiable anger is always in vogue. Voice mail is just cause for temper tantrums. If you ever get past "Press one now" and "Press two for service" and actually get a human voice on the line, tell him or her just how you feel about being shunted about by a recording, then being disconnected and having to start all over again with the same results. Complain loudly that voice mail is like being in purgatory, whirling about endlessly in limbo. Say you will not do business with their firm anymore. Of course, if it's medicare you're yelling at, you might as well be in purgatory.

Greed is just another word for survival. For years we've been accumulating Social Security, lottery tickets, Mother's tea set, and other valuables. Now, in our seniority, prices outstrip our income, and taxes leave us in a negative cash flow. Banks offer us reverse mortgages on our home, allowing us to live in our own house, now mortgage free, with a monthly payment from the bank. When we die, the bank gets the house. This is greed? How else are we going to pay for our Early Bird dinners?

Gluttony is not something oldies worry about. The contemporary dietary dogma is so complex, we've given up and gone back to eating anything we want. If we adhered to all the contemporary dietary restrictions, we couldn't be gluttonous if we tried. Remember when cookies and milk were the health foods we gave our children after school? Now whole milk is fatal, and so are cookies. Eggs might give us salmonella. Cream of tomato soup is too salty to be considered, and hamburger, the all-American staple, will congeal your innards. Some oldies, like former President George Bush, even suspect broccoli. Apples have frightened us. The only two things still permitted are (1) hot chili peppers to stimulate our endorphins or (2) a glass of wine to keep our arteries open. (Whoever wanted *one* glass of wine?)

Envy is alive and well. We envy young, svelte bodies and shiny hair. That's about it. We do not envy struggling to get an education and finding no jobs available when we graduate. We do not envy having small children who whine and let their noses run. Getting up at 5 A.M. to go to work and then rushing home only to do the laundry at night is not attractive to us. We like being old. It's easier.

Lust, like vanity, never dies. Oldies are still prowling around wondering how they are going to relieve their sexual tensions. Lust is a characteristic that we share with animals. Animals are superior to and have advantages over humans. In addition to being better-looking, more efficient, and more honest, animals don't know they are going to die, and they suffer lust only seasonally.

Sloth is a luxury. Latter-day sloth allows us to forbid out-of-town visitors to stay in our homes. We're too lazy. We have finally learned to reserve a room in a motel for them. And how sweet it is to drop them off at the departing flights gate at the airport and then drive home blissfully free. Sloth is the reward of the old for the guilt, the "shoulds," and the "oughts" we have suffered all our lives. We have finally given up guilt. We have learned that if it hurts no one, do it. Or better yet, don't do it. Now we have choices.

Mixed Emotions

I saw a cartoon about death the other day. It was *Arlo and Janis* by Jimmy Johnson (NEA, Inc.). In the cartoon, one of Arlo's friends has died. Arlo tells his wife the friend, who was his own age, died of a heart attack eating lobster in a Tahitian bar. Arlo looks stricken. But then, in the last drawing, Arlo looks puzzled and says, "My emotions are mixed."

I think that's the way a lot of us feel about death. At our age, we are going to more funerals than we used to. When it is our nearest and dearest, the grief is profound and is probably all we feel. People say they feel paralyzed, that it takes two years before they begin to stabilize, and even then the grief and loneliness is not fully gone.

When a parent goes, we might be relieved because we have had the care and worry during a long illness. At the end of life, we'd like it to just be over, not to linger. My father died after years of Alzheimer's disease. When he was finally gone, I felt that I had already grieved for him for five years. At his death I felt only relief, even gratitude that it was finally over for him. My grief had been used up.

But when someone our age dies—not our spouse or child, but a friend—and dies easily, without a long illness, we feel sad at first, then a sneaky little thought slips in. *He was lucky. I hope I can go as easily.*

At funerals, we sometimes look around at other people our age and think, *Who will be next? There's old what's-her-name. I haven't seen her since she retired. She's aged a lot. Will it be her? Will it be me?* This is scary.

Sometimes we aren't sad at all. When someone dies who has been a trial, someone we did not like, maybe even hated in our uncharitable moments, our feeling might be, well, glad. I admit to hiding behind the obituary page and smiling a little private smile to myself.

And everyone knows that a lot of laughing goes on at funerals. Yes, it relieves tension. But also, we are happy that it wasn't our turn yet.

So, when I read the *Arlo and Janis* cartoon, I understood. Death stimulates mixed emotions. And we feel puzzled.

I Saw an Owl Today

A friend told me of walking through a Florida state park and first seeing an owl, then hearing it. "It was a large bird," she said, "at least twelve inches tall, beige and brown in a herringbone pattern."

Then it flew. "I knew," she said, "that owls fly silently, but I never knew the true meaning of that silence until I saw, but could not hear, the bird descend—soft and deadly—and disappear into the woods. I wish," she said, "that when we report our day, we could say more often, 'I saw an owl today,' rather than 'the traffic was unbearable' or 'I was overcharged.'"

I was in a wooded area recently, near enough to city traffic to hear cars on the freeway, but even that close to chaos, I saw several deer, sandhill cranes, a small alligator, and footprints that might have been a bobcat's. In the lambent shade of cypress, I saw plants called pennywort, hatpin, pond spice, and sundew—a small, rosy carnivorous plant.

On a back highway, another day, we had to slow the car to avoid peacocks, arrogantly sweeping the road dust with their impossible tails. We have to slow on city streets also because wild Muscovy ducks think duck traffic has the right-of-way. And they are right.

Even in the city, animals are all around us. At dawn, there are more birdcalls than I can count. Raccoons and opossums would move in with us if they were invited—and sometimes do, whether they are invited or not. Porpoises and mullet leap in Tampa Bay. Snakes and turtles are common; squirrels and other rodents are all over town.

Animals have always been important to us, but I think as we get older, we regain a childlike capacity for observation. Or maybe our mortality is becoming a reality, and we savor life more precisely.

I love to see horses in a field, cavorting without saddles or bridles. When I see dogs running in the park in a group, I get a warm, happy feeling. Domestic animals love to be free of human harnessing. Sometimes I see a large dog straining at his leash, his master insisting that he heel. The dog wants to be a dog, but the owner wants him to behave like a human.

Our household pets become family. Our children grow up and leave home, but the cat is still there, needing to be fed and petted every day. A dog or cat or bird is a reason to get up and dress in the morning. The animals need food, a door opened, a walk. I read somewhere that many older people are never touched, except by their doctors and their pets. The dog or cat is warm and soft and a good friend, someone to talk to.

Animals are so important to us that if we don't have real ones, we resort to stuffed toy ones. Our parents know this. After my mother moved into a retirement home alone, she bought herself a large teddy bear. I know of at least five other people who have recently purchased teddy bears, not for grandchildren or great-grandchildren, but to hold themselves.

Both wild and domestic animals refresh our spirit. They remind us that we are part of the natural world. Those of us who live in cities sometimes begin to feel like machines rather than the mammals we are. It is rare that we can report: "I saw an owl today."

The Journey Continues

December is the time of year to think of beginnings and endings, new years and old, of the cycles of nature and the cycles of life.

In my family there is a one-year-old granddaughter, Autumn Rain, and an eighty-six-year old grandmother, Ella. My mother is at the end of her cycle, bedridden now with cancer of the spine. She is often confused, perhaps by pain medication, and sometimes she thinks I am still a child. Other times she asks if anyone is taking care of Pa—her father who died forty years ago. Like most women, she worries that her children and parents are cared for.

Autumn is just beginning her journey through life, traveling quickly on sturdy legs, her little square body healthy and strong. A child of the nineties, she was born cynical and opinionated. Wary, she already knows the world is a suspicious place and complains loudly if she suspects she is to be separated from her mother for even an hour or two. Her mother is a known quantity: comforting, safe, and beautiful.

I took another kind of journey last month, a train trip across the northern United States. As we traveled west, we had a series of three twenty-five-hour days while the train tried to keep up with the sun's cycles.

The trek across North Dakota was especially poignant because that is where my mother and I were born. The city names were those of my childhood: Fargo, Minot, Devils Lake. I was born in Carrington, in the front bedroom at Grandma's house. That done, Grandma—Anna Marie—gave me my first bath in a basin on the kitchen table.

Papier-Mache Press

At Papier-Mache Press, it is our goal to identify and successfully present important social issues through enduring works of beauty, grace, and strength. Through our work we hope to encourage empathy and respect among diverse communities, creating a bridge of understanding between the mainstream audience and those who might not otherwise be heard.

We appreciate you, our customer, and strive to earn your continued support. We also value the role of the bookseller in achieving our goals. We are especially grateful to the many independent booksellers whose presence ensures a continuing diversity of opinion, information, and literature in our communities. We encourage you to support these bookstores with your patronage.

We publish many fine books about women's experiences. We also produce lovely posters and T-shirts that complement our anthologies. Please ask your local bookstore which Papier-Mache items they carry. To receive our complete catalog, send a self-addressed stamped envelope to Papier-Mache Press, 135 Aviation Way, #14, Watsonville, CA 95076, or call our toll-free number, 800-927-5913.

About the Author

Niela Eliason worked for many years as a registered nurse after graduating from St. Luke's Hospital School of Nursing in Denver, Colorado. She returned to college at midlife, receiving a bachelor's degree in English from the University of South Florida in 1980. She then began writing, starting with a letter to the editor. Now a freelance writer, she has written an essay column for the *St. Petersburg Times* for ten years. She has been writing her "Fiftysomething" and "Sixtysomething" columns for the last four years. Eliason, now sixtysomething, lives with her husband in St. Petersburg, Florida.

Last month, as the train followed the curve of the earth across the northern states, I thought of Anna Marie and Ella and Autumn and the continuity of life from grandmother to mother, daughter, and grand-daughter. We move through the seasons of life just as the sun makes its revolutions and the years make full circles from spring to winter.

The train whistle sounded at the front of the train, full of both hope and caution, announcing our movement across the continent. The wintry great plains were dusted with snow, the land silver and gold with harvested grain. Bare trees made black silhouettes of lace against the white sky. The plains passed the train window, mile after mile, and turned pearl white and pink at sundown as the train continued to hurtle day and night across the continent toward California where the trip would end.

Nature insists on closures, beginnings and endings. My mother is hearing the whistle warning her of her journey's end. Autumn is just taking her first eager steps. I am somewhere between, about three-quarters of the way through my life cycle. Still strong and vigorous, I cannot see the inexorable conclusion of my journey. But no matter. All I need to know is that the sun will rise tomorrow, the tides and seasons will change, Autumn will grow and fulfill her destiny. I am here for this period of time to observe, to learn and enjoy, to contribute what I can, and to complete my own cycle while the whistle sounds eerily, proceed-ing ahead, somewhere in the future.